The Secret:
SUCCESSFUL
BUSINESS
REPORT
WRITING

About the author

Born in Edgware, Middlesex, longer ago than he dares to think about, **Clive Goodworth** was for twenty years a regular officer in the Royal Air Force. In 1968 he joined the Road Transport Industry Training Board as a training adviser where he spent two years before becoming a senior personnel executive with an international oil company. In 1975 he went into teaching and became Senior Lecturer in Management and Professional Studies at the Huntingdonshire College. A few years ago he decided to devote himself to full-time writing.

Books in the series

The Secrets of
SUCCESSFUL
BUSINESS
REPORT
WRITING

Clive Goodworth

BUTTERWORTH
HEINEMANN

Butterworth-Heinemann Ltd
Halley Court, Jordan Hill, Oxford OX2 8EJ

PART OF REED INTERNATIONAL BOOKS

OXFORD   LONDON   GUILDFORD   BOSTON
MUNICH   NEW DELHI   SINGAPORE   SYDNEY
TOKYO   TORONTO   WELLINGTON

First published 1991

British Library Cataloguing in Publication Data
Goodworth, Clive T.
   The secrets of successful business report writing.
   1. Reports. Compilation
   I. Title
   808.06665

ISBN 0 7506 0031 4

Photoset by Deltatype Ltd, Ellesmere Port, Cheshire
Printed in Great Britain by
Billings & Sons, Worcester

Dedicated to all those unsung heroes who, like me, have suffered the slings and arrows of the reporting battlefield. I hope this helps!

Contents

Figures

1 First things first

> They have committed false report; moreover, they have
> written untruths; secondarily, they are libels; sixth and lastly,
> they have belied a lady; thirdly, they have verified unjust
> things; and to conclude, they are lying knaves.
>
> With apologies to William Shakespeare

Since you've been brave enough to start reading this
stuff, I reckon it's an odds-on bet that the mere thought of
having to write a report is enough to make your toes curl. If
this is so, take a crumb of comfort – first, in the knowledge
that you share your aversion with a whole army of fellow-
sufferers; second, in the fact that your report-writing malaise
is not, repeat not, incurable; and, third, in my assurance that
right in front of your eyes is the very prescription to bring
about at least some of that cure.

No, hold on – before you slam your mental door in my face,
I'm going to jam my size eleven therein and pose a couple of
questions . . . In seeking a book on report writing, would you
really prefer a kind of instant crib bank – a handy first-aid kit,
to which you can fly for help whenever the need arises? Or is it
the case that you're the studious type, who actually wishes to
learn all about the subject with the help of a flamin' textbook?
Well, the good news is, it doesn't matter a tinker's cuss – for
the simple reason that this book is expressly designed to meet
both of these needs. So, before we kick off with some scene-
setting food for thought, perhaps you'd like to store this little
gem in your noddle:

- For the crib bank approach, merely fly to the Index – look
  up whatever's relevant, and knock that report into shape
  the easy way.
- For the studious approach, note that each chapter ends
  with a Workbox for your attention, together with an

associated Tutorial. The message is simple – there's more than enough to keep you occupied, so get slogging!

Hello and welcome. It's an undeniable fact that the vast majority of us dislike writing reports – and, if we're strictly honest, often regard such work with an element of fear. There are a number of very good reasons for this; not least among them being the unpalatable truth that, in this so-called technological age, the centuries-old craft of written communication is, sadly, a dying craft. But, whatever the reason, we have to accept that a whole army of Jack and Jill desk pilots find it difficult enough to compile an internal memo, let alone a report. At the risk of appearing unduly cynical, we've almost reached the stage where it's possible to coin a standard drill for the report-writing task; to wit:

1   When the need to write a report does arise, DON'T. This overall and vital objective may be achieved by:
  - qualifying as a black belt procrastinator;
  - resolutely delegating anything and everything that smacks of the dreaded chore;
  - quietly passing the word that one suffers from Feudenkilstein's Intermittent Dyslexia;
  - ensuring spontaneous combustion of one's in-tray.

2   When all else fails, go sick – preferably in the Orkneys.
You won't need reminding that things weren't always like this. In those halcyon times before our twentieth-century gadgetry peeled the vital need for written communication like an orange, managers *had* to write many, many reports. What's more, if their multifarious efforts are anything to go by, a significant proportion of 'em were not only good at the art – they positively enjoyed it. Tell you what, let's resurrect just a few of those bygone jewels of the written word.

For clarity, brevity and sheer excellence of impact, consider that all-time winner of a report written by Julius Caesar (100–44 BC) at the conclusion of his victorious Pontic campaign:

Veni, vedi, vici

which, as every schoolboy used to know, translates into those immortal words:

I came, I saw, I conquered

The Venerable Bede (AD 673–735), a redoubtable English historian, was a dab hand at journalistic reporting. Writing on the burial-place of St Chad, he commented thus on a somewhat dubious but popular practice:

> . . . the place of the sepulchre is a wooden monument, made like a little house, covered, having a hole in the wall, through which those that go thither for devotion usually put in their hand and take out some of the dust, which they put into water and give to sick cattle or men to drink, upon which they are presently eased of their infirmity, and restored to health.
>
> (Giles, Dr transl. (1843). Bede, *Historia Ecclesiastica Gentis Anglorum*. London)

Swinging up through the ages to the time of Henry Plantagenet (1133–1189), one Peter of Blois, an intimate of the king, reported amusingly on the manner in which his sovereign delighted in playing havoc with the arrangements for this or that royal progression:

> If the King had promised to remain in a place for that day – and especially if he had announced his intention publicly by the mouth of a herald – he is sure to upset all the arrangements by departing early in the morning. As a result, you see men dashing around as if they were mad, beating their packhorses, running their carts into one another – in short, giving a lively imitation of Hell. If, on the other hand, the King orders an early start, he is certain to change his mind, and you can take it for granted that he will sleep until midday. Then you will see the packhorses loaded and waiting, the carts prepared, the courtiers dozing, traders fretting and everyone grumbling . . . When our couriers had gone ahead almost the whole day's ride, the King would turn aside to some other place where he had, it might be, just a single house with accommodation for himself and no one else. I hardly dare say it, but I believe that in truth he took a delight in seeing what a fix he put us in. After wandering some three or four miles in an unknown wood, and often in the dark, we thought ourselves lucky if we stumbled upon some filthy little hovel. There was often *a sharp* and bitter argument about a mere hut, and swords were drawn for possession of a lodging which pigs would have shunned.
>
> Giles, J.A. (Ed) (1848). *Epistolae, Peter of Blois*. London)

In 1773, when William Pitt the Younger (a boy wonder if there ever was one) attained the ripe old age of 14, he was packed off to Pembroke Hall, Cambridge to obtain a degree. Reporting on the decision to send him there, his tutor wrote:

> I could not have acted with more prudence than I have done in the affair of Pembroke Hall. Mr Pitt is not the child his years bespeak him to be. He has now all the understanding of a man. He has sound principles, a grateful and liberal heart, and talents unequalled. He will go to Pembroke, not a weak boy to be made a property of, but to be admired as a prodigy; not to hear lectures but to spread light. His parts are most astonishing and universal. He will be perfectly qualified for a wrangler before he goes, and will be an accomplished classick, mathematician, historian and poet. This is no exaggeration.
>
> Ehrmann, J. (1970). *The Younger Pitt: The Years of Acclaim*. Dutton

And, as events turned out, it wasn't . . .

It has been said that it took the Victorians to mould written English into a dignified and expressive art form. While today's push-button-bred reader may condemn their general style as one of florid and needless extravagance, there is little doubt that the reporters of that era were, indeed, dignified and expressive. Consider, if you will, three extracts from a report penned in October 1840 by the engineering genius, Isambard Kingdom Brunel, on the subject of that enduring vessel, *Great Britain:*

> Gentlemen, I have now the pleasure to lay before you the result of the different experiments which I have made and of the best consideration I have been able to give to the subject of the screw propeller.
>
> The observations which I have to make are naturally devised under two principal heads – namely – first the simple question of the applicability and efficiency of the screw considered merely as a means of propelling a vessel compared with the ordinary paddle wheel and secondly the general advantages or disadvantages attending its use.

and

> A clean run is the most essential condition and I should suppose no ship was ever built in which this principle of form was carried to a greater extent than in our new Iron Ship – Her present form I believe to be excellent for the screw and with the very slight dropping of the keel towards the stern which can easily be done now without any expense, assisted by the

different trim which I shall presently show will be affected by the use of the screw the required draught of water will be attained.

and, lastly

From all that I have said it must be evident to you Gentlemen that my opinion is strong and decidedly in favour of the advantage of employing the screw in the new ship – it certainly is so. I am fully aware of the responsibilities I take upon myself by giving this advice.

> Brunel, I. (1870). *The Life of*
> *Isambard Brunel.* London

T'was in 1864 that a sadly anonymous Victorian businessman found himself bound to write what I fondly regard as a masterpiece of report understatement to his partner in France:

. . . as a consequence of these continued misfortunes, we no longer enjoy our good standing at the Bank. I require to issue drafts, but dare not. Our creditors press with a vigour that betokens their full knowledge of our parlous affairs – and Mr Pusey, our new Landlord, is in daily attendance at the Office, seeking his rightful dues. I have been obliged to dispense with the services of Jos Booker, our loyal and diligent Clerk – and Edward has yet to receive wages in respect of the week ending 25th. and thereafter. Unless and until you can see yr way to returning with the promised monies by the earliest Packet, **I must confess that I entertain some small doubt as to our future.**

> Copy of a letter, signature illegible, discovered in an
> old tin box containing documents accumulated by
> my late grandfather, F. A. Goodworth.

I can think of no better example with which to round off this glimpse of bygone reportage than a snippet from the log kept by Ernest Shackleton, that intrepid pathfinder to the South Pole. On 20 November 1908 he wrote of earth's most fearsome waste:

The whole place seems so strange and unlike anything else in the world . . . when the hazy clouds spring silently from either hand and drift quickly across our zenith not followed by any wind it seems almost uncanny. Then comes a puff of wind . . . seeming to obey no law acting on erratic impulses. It seems as though we were truly at the world's end and were bursting in on the birthplace of the clouds and the nesting home of the four winds and that we mortals were being watched with a jealous eye by these children of Nature.

> Shackleton, Sir E. (1909). *The Heart of the Antarctic.* London

All right. Having subjected you to a spot of nostalgic reminiscence, we now have to slide with a mighty bump into the present day and pose an important, square-one question – in order that we can get our subject into some form of perspective, what are the various meanings of the verb 'report'? Cast your eye over the following definitions:

1 To bear or bring back as an answer; repeat; relate, as information obtained by an investigation – *hence, to give an account of.*
2 *To state as a fact*; circulate publicly; tell, as a story.
3 *To prepare from personal observation or inquiry a more or less detailed record of, usually for publication*; to serve as a reporter.
4 To certify formally or officially a result, condition or situation; as, he *reports* the balance of an account.
5 One not to be forgotten – to inform against before a superior; as, to *report* a subordinate for this or that transgression.

There are some further definitions, but they're concerned with the verbal side of reporting – which wide-ranging subject is thankfully outside our terms of reference.

Having thus tapped the foundation-stone into place, it now behoves us to take a long, hard look at the first practical aspect of dealing with written reports – the business of arranging them into types or classes.

The classification of written reports

Before tackling the classification of reports by content, there are a few overall considerations to be taken into account. First, there is the question of the form in which a report, any report, is to be presented. While often there will be no choice in the matter, it's worth remembering that a report can take two forms:

1   *Letter/memorandum form*   Do not run away with the idea (as if you would) that a report written in the form of a letter or memorandum smacks of arrant informality – whatever Big Daddy may say to the contrary and always provided the wording is right, it doesn't. If the subject matter of a particular report is simple and limited in scope, the letter or memorandum can be more than adequate as a vehicle for one's formal *tour de force*.

For an example of a letter-type report, see page 40. For an example of a memo-type report, see page 15.

It is when the subject matter demands a more complex and lengthy treatment that the wise reporter will turn to the alternative – see below.

2   *Full schematic presentation*   In this form of report, the subject matter is divided into easily recognizable sections and subsections, with title headings and subheadings (pure Whitehallese, this) strategically positioned throughout the text. In other words, the accent is on logical presentation and ease of reference.

To follow up schematic presentation, turn to page 25.

Now for the classification of reports by content – and, no, I do not wish to be reminded that you've produced a masterpiece of report writing which cannot be categorized under any of the following headings. Merely give yourself a pat on the back, you inventive son-of-a-gun, and stop making a fuss about nothing.

1   *Single or ad hoc reports*   These are reports on matters or

situations which, by their very nature, are of limited scope and/or duration – and, hence, can be adequately covered within a single document.

For examples of single reports, see pages 30, 40.

2   *Progress reports*   Self-explanatory or not, let's spell it out. These are periodic reports on ongoing ventures; detailing progress towards given objectives, snags and hiccups encountered on the way, successes and failures to date, and so on.

For an example of a progress report, see page 89.

3   *Completion reports*   Yes, you've got it in one – the final document in a series of progress reports, detailing the glorious (hurray) or inglorious (yuk) outcome of the venture concerned.

For an example of the contents table of acompletion report, see page 37.

4   *Routine reports*   Almost any organization with a smidgen of bureaucracy in its corporate veins has a positive yen for routine reports – for, without 'em, how on earth would those denizens of middle and senior management rest easy o'nights? It is perhaps fortunate that most routine reports

are required to be rendered on preprinted forms – so, apart from the oft-complicated and infinitely risky practice of embroidering the figures, they should present little in the way of trouble to the originator. Nuff said.

5 *Investigation reports*   Again, these reports are pretty self-explanatory; in-depth investigation-cum-analyses – invariably culminating in reasoned conclusions and/or recommendations on specific courses of action.

For an example of an investigation report, see page 89.

6 *Eye-witness reports*   In a sense, these are the gloom-and-doom merchants in the report collection, for they are nearly always associated with accidents and other misfortunes.

For an example of the main body of an eye-witness report, see page 53.

Quo vadis?

In the next chapter, we go straight to the first slice of meat in the report writing sandwich – a detailed, step-by-step examination of two most important aspects of our study, the techniques of format and display. However, since you've stuck with me thus far, I'm going to assume that you are, indeed, a studious type – so, first, there's the small matter of Workbox Number 1 to be completed.

Workbox 1

You will probably roar through this initial workbox like a dose of salts, but don't succumb to the thought that they're *all* going to be as simple as this one, will you? We've scarcely started, yet . . .

Remembering that reports can be classified as:

- Single or *ad hoc* reports
- Progress reports
- Completion reports
- Routine reports
- Investigation reports
- Eye-witness reports

Examine the following list of report titles, and have a go at classifying each one.

1 Interim Report on the Installation of a New Drainage System at the Desborough 'A' Site.
2 The Use of Open Learning in Management Development Programmes: Report of a Working Party under the Chairmanship of Professor T. M. Klauswitz.
3 New Layout for the Epsom Branch Reception Area.
4 US Congress, House of Representatives: House Report No 354, 44th Congress, 1st Session, Volume 2, 1876, Serial 1760. Reduction of Officers' Pay, Reorganization of the Army, and Transfer of the Indian Bureau.
5 Lord Devlin, Chairman, Committee of Inquiry into the Port Transport Industry – Final Report.
6 Loss of HMS Royal Oak – Board of Inquiry Sub-committee of the Board, Survivors' Statements.
7 Regional Manager's Monthly Report.

> 8 Report by D. H. Williams, Asst. Air Traffic Control-
> ler, on the Accident Involving DH Dove Aircraft
> GA–XYZ at Hurn Airport on 15 February 1989.

Tutorial to Workbox 1

Well, now, I reckon it's likely that you found this wee exercise
a little less straightforward than you expected; not least, for
the reason that some of the titles tend to pitchfork one into the
many grey areas of report classification – and, hence, into the
hoary old, time-wasting game of semantics. Be that as it may,
here are my thoughts on the task.

1 An interim report on a project – so, yes, this is a *progress
  report*.
2 Since working parties are invariably set up to deal with
  specific issues, I'd suggest that this example can be
  classified as a *single* or *ad hoc report*.
3 On the limited evidence available, another *single* or *ad hoc
  report*.
4 I think the clue to this one is contained in the words,
  'House Report No 354'. While the subject of the report
  may prompt one to classify it as yet another *single* or *ad hoc*
  example, the US House of Representatives' Reports are of
  the same ilk as our own Parliamentary Hansard; i.e. issued
  on a regular basis. So I'd offer that this is a *routine report*.
5 The final report of a committee of inquiry is plainly a
  completion report.
6 Cutting through the Whitehall verbiage, a 'Sub-
  Committee of the Board' is, in essence, just another term
  for a working party – so, from that angle, this example
  would appear to be classifiable as a *single* or *ad hoc report*.
  However, when our eyes turn to the subject matter,
  survivors' statements, we could hardly be blamed for
  classifying this document as an *eye-witness report*. While it
  may upset the purist at heart, I'd be happy with either
  alternative.
7 Hum, just picture in your mind's eye the poor old regional
  manager flogging his way through yet another *routine
  report*.

8   There's little doubt about this one, I think – an *eye-witness report*.

So there we are, a gentle let-down for your first workbox. Now, I recommend that you equip yourself with a refreshing cuppa-cum-noggin – for as sure as the Great Chairman in the Sky made little apples, you're going to need it.

2   The essential questions of format and display

> Keep up appearances; there lies the test;
> The world will give thee credit for the rest.
> Outward be fair, however foul within;
> Sin if thou wilt, but then in secret sin.
>
>   Charles Churchill (1731–1764), 'Night'

It's a truism that all managers are different, and even more of a truism that the myriad reports produced by 'em are different – and that, reader, is one hell of an understatement. Ask your run-of-the-mill executive pen-pusher about the format of a typical report, and it's more than likely that the response will bounce along time-hallowed lines:

Ho, hum – format of a typical report, y'say . . . Well, now, I s'pose it's got to have a title of some sort of another . . . [The glazed look on the speaker's face is indicative of a headlong plunge into frenetic mental activity.] *And, er, it'll have to come up with something at the end . . .* [Wait for it – nothing less than a revelation is threatening to burst upon the scene.] *Aha, yes, I know . . .* [And, suddenly, he does.] *That's it – recommendations!* [Triumphantly] *There you are, then . . .*

As I'm sure you realize, there's a bit more to formats than that – so, let's stop mucking about and take a long, hard look at this vital aspect of report writing.

Format of the informal report

For an example of the beginning of an informal report, see page 40.

PANIC BUTTON

The informal report is normally used when the information to be supplied is lacking in complexity and is of such an order that it would be gilding the lily to render it in formal style. For this reason, it is frequently utilized by those who occupy slots at or near the base of the organization pyramid, i.e., when the supervisor or junior manager writes a report to his or her immediate boss. Mind you, many senior managers seem to be under the impression that to produce an informal report would somehow undermine their precious status – and they do their best to wrap even the most trivial topic in stultifying, armour-plated formality.

The most convenient vehicle for an informal report which is destined for 'internal' circulation is the ubiquitous memorandum – usually preprinted, with a handy, ready-made heading, as shown in Figure 1.

MEMORANDUM

| To: | Date: |
| From: | Ref: |

Subject:

Figure 1   A typical memorandum heading

Note, if you will, the item 'Ref:' in Figure 1, and forgive my mentioning that it is simply not good enough either to leave the space blank, *or* to have your secretary or typist slap down your and her initials (e.g. DFG/CB) as a reference. The object of a file reference system is to enable documents to be (a) logically collated by subject, and (b) readily located in their respective files. The widespread practice of blazoning one's own initials as a reference is not only a sign of poor administration, but is entirely superfluous to boot. After all, they're there for everyone to see in the 'From:' subheading and, hopefully, are also plain from one's signature. As for the typist's initials, if it is absolutely essential to have them, put

---

MEMORANDUM

To: Date:

From: Ref:

Subject:

COMPONENT 1   This opening section (which may or may not include <u>headed</u> paragraph(s) – the choice is yours) should comprise the <u>introduction</u> to the informal report: an acknowledgement of the instructions for the task; any amplification of the subject heading considered necessary; background or situation details, etc.

COMPONENT 2   This section should comprise the 'main body' of the informal report: information, findings, etc. Note, again, that headings to paragraphs are optional.

COMPONENT 3   This final section should comprise details of any action required; conclusions and/or recommendations, etc.

NOTE that abbreviations are entirely permissible and often desirable within memos, <u>provided it is certain that the recipient(s) will understand them.</u>

Figure 2   The format of an informal report

'em somewhere else – and devise a proper file reference system, pronto.

Figure 2 goes a stage further, and depicts the principal components of the 'text format' for this type of report.

Format of the short formal report

For an example of a short formal report, see page 30.

Yes, I know what you're thinking, one person's 'short' is another person's interminably long; so I'll do my best to explain. The vast majority of formal reporting situations within business and industry entail the production by middle/senior managers of, say, two- to ten-page reports (one cannot be more precise than that) for their bosses – and I can think of no better way to describe this category than 'short'.

Having wriggled round that one, I'd like to remind you that the formal style of report should be utilized only after due thought. While some (but by no means all) civil servants and sundry other bureaucrats may regard the submission of an informal report as little short of *lèse-majesté*, such an attitude is strictly for the birds. The thinking report writer will always weigh the nature and complexity of the given subject before leaping precipitately into formalese – especially when his or her ability to communicate in writing, anyway, is a bit on the shaky side.

The principal components of the short formal report

(a) Routing and administrative details (addressee[s]; file reference; security classification, if any)

For info on referencing/numbering see page 22.

(b)   Subject heading or title

For info on
headings/titles,
see page 34.

(c)   Terms of reference

For info on
terms of
reference,
see page 38.

(d)   Introduction

For info on
introductions,
see page 52.

(e)   Main body

For lots on the
main body of a
report, see
page 59.

(f)   Findings/conclusions

For info on
findings/
conclusions,
see page 82.

(g)   Recommendations

For info on
recommendations,
see page 86.

(h)

Appendices, if any

For info on
appendices,
see page 88.

Format of the long/complex formal report

For an example of
a long/complex
formal report,
see page 89.

And now we're into the lip-smacking, *crème de la crème* of the report writing world – the oft-convoluted and always complex, heavyweight document spawned by those who, more often than not, squat way above us in the hot-seats of power. However, Sod's Law being what it is, there will always be the odd, fateful occasion when you and I will be required to produce such a beast – so here goes.

The principal components of the long/complex formal report

(a) Title page, including
     routing and administrative
     details (addressee[s];
     file reference; security
     classification, if any)

For
info on
these
points,
see page 34.

(b) Contents list with page
     numbers

For info on
contents lists,
see page 37.

(c)
     Terms of reference

For info on terms
of reference
see page 38.

(d) Brief summary of main
     body and synopsis of
     findings

For info on
these points,
see page 45.

(e) Introduction, if appropriate

For info on
introductions,
see page 52.

(f)
　　Main body

　　　　　　　For lots on the
　　　　　　　main body of a
　　　　　report, see page 59.

(g)　Itemized findings

　　　　　　For an example of findings,
　　　　　　　　　　see page 69.

(h)　Itemized conclusions

　　　　　　　For info on conclusions,
　　　　　　　　　　see page 82.

(i)　Itemized recommendations

　　　　　　　　　For info on
　　　　　recommendations,
　　　　　　　　see page 86.

(j)　Appendices, if any

　　　　　　　For info on
　　　　　appendices,
　　　　　see page 88.

(k) Bibliography and/or
     acknowledgements,
     if any

For info on
these points,
see page 99.

And now we come to an aspect of our study which, in some degree or other, is common to all types of report, however presented; namely:

SUMMARY OF FINDINGS

The existing arrangements within the Avionics Division for the assessment and notification to employees of rates of pay, including basic scales applicable to those on incentive or other bonus schemes, are highly questionable. The major areas for concern can be summarized as follows:

frequent failure by recruiting managers to assess realistic commencing rates of pay;

an associated failure by those responsible to ensure that commencing rates of pay awarded in respect of identical jobs are standardized throughout the Division;

despite repeated representations by members of the Works Council; a continuing failure by management to implement a visibly effective system for the annual review of:

wages and salaries;

incentive and other bonus schemes;

travel and other allowances;

an almost total adherence to a policy of secrecy in relation to the rates of remuneration for office workers throughout the Division.

Figure 3   Sample of text without referencing/numbering

Referencing/numbering systems

If you'll bear with me, I'm going to utilize the same piece of text several times within this section as a means of illustrating the various approaches to this important question of referencing/numbering paragraphs, sub-paragraphs and so on. What I'd like *you* to do is simply inspect each version and make up your own mind which system is best suited to your particular requirements. But, first, take a look at Figure 3.

---

8   SUMMARY OF FINDINGS

The existing arrangements within the Avionics Division for the assessment and notification to employees of rates of pay, including basic scales applicable to those on incentive or other bonus schemes, are highly questionable. The major areas for concern can be summarized as follows:

(a) frequent failure by recruiting managers to assess realistic commencing rates of pay;

(b) an associated failure by those responsible to ensure that commencing rates of pay awarded in respect of identical jobs are standardized throughout the Division;

(c) despite repeated representations by members of the Works Council, a continuing failure by management to implement a visibly effective system for the annual review of:

   (i)   wages and salaries;
   (ii)   incentive and other bonus schemes;
   (iii) travel and other allowances;

(d) an almost total adherence to a policy of secrecy in relation to the rates of remuneration for office workers throughout the Division.

Figure 4   The sample text with the main section, subsections and subordinate points identified by means of an arabic numeral, lower case letters in brackets and lower case roman numerals, respectively

One of the basic requirements of any report containing more than a couple of paragraphs is that the recipient should be able to 'tag' (i.e. have a means of referring to) any particular items of importance or interest. Our very short sample text in Figure 3 is devoid of any referencing/numbering and, if we regard it as an extract from a longer document, I think you'll agree that it would be a tedious job, indeed, to make handy reference to any specific point. Furthermore, if when compiling the thing, the writer wished to refer to an earlier paragraph, sentence, etc., he or she would find it quite difficult to do so without some form of numbering/referencing. Now take a look at Figure 4.

H   SUMMARY OF FINDINGS

The existing arrangements within the Avionics Division for the assessment and notification to employees of rates of pay, including basic scales applicable to those on incentive or other bonus schemes, are highly questionable. The major areas for concern can be summarized as follows:

1   frequent failure by recruiting managers to assess realistic commencing rates of pay;
2   an associated failure by those responsible to ensure that commencing rates of pay awarded in respect of identical jobs are standardized throughout the Division;
3   despite repeated representations by members of the Works Council, a continuing failure by management to implement a visibly effective system for the annual review of:
  (a)   wages and salaries;
  (b)   incentive and other bonus schemes;
  (c)   travel and other allowances;
4   an almost total adherence to a policy of secrecy in relation to the rates of remuneration for office workers throughout the Division.

Figure 5   The sample text with the main section, subsections and subordinate points identified by means of a capital letter, arabic numerals, and lower case letters in brackets, respectively

I hope you will agree that Figure 4 presents our sample text in a much more orderly way. Certainly, if one wished to call attention to the subordinate point 'wages and salaries', it is now only necessary to refer to 'para 3(c)(i)' and, hey presto, it's done. This isn't an attempt on my part to swamp you with administrative gobbledegook; it makes good, sound common sense – and if you wish to succeed with your report writing, you'd better believe it!

Just to make life interesting, there are several alternative ways of playing the numbering/referencing game – and

---

8   SUMMARY OF FINDINGS

The existing arrangements within the Avionics Division for the assessment and notification to employees of rates of pay, including basic scales applicable to those on incentive or other bonus schemes, are highly questionable. The major areas for concern can be summarized as follows:

8.1   frequent failure by recruiting managers to assess realistic commencing rates of pay;

8.2   an associated failure by those responsible to ensure that commencing rates of pay awarded in respect of identical jobs are standardized throughout the Division;

8.3   despite repeated representations by members of the Works Council, a continuing failure by management to implement a visibly effective system for the annual review of:

8.3.1   wages and salaries;
8.3.2   incentive and other bonus schemes;
8.3.3   travel and other allowances;

8.4   an almost total adherence to a policy of secrecy in relation to the rates of remuneration for office workers throughout the Division.

Figure 6   The sample text with the main section, subsections and subordinate points identified by means of a straightforward numbering system (note the full stop 'separations'). This method is much favoured by those in government departments

Figures 5 and 6 depict two of these. It's really a matter of yer pays yer money, yer takes yer choice . . .

Getting the display right

Many moons ago, I worked alongside a guy who was the absolute bee's knees at tackling reports. Throw old George the most complicated task under the sun and, in no time flat, he'd have the subject mentally reviewed and analysed – with well-nigh perfect text spouting from his computer of a brain like water from a tap. The only trouble was, he just didn't have a clue when it came to display; and, in the total absence of any guidance from her otherwise excellent boss, George's secretary was left to churn out his reports as best she could. Almost invariably the result was that the products of this flint-sharp executive mind were presented as off-putting, rock-solid masses of words – which, despite their intrinsic quality, caused many a reader bags of frustration and annoyance.

So the moral is, having got the words and the numbering/referencing right, make jolly certain that the finished article is not wholly indigestible to the eye.

Some tips on display

1 Always make *full* use of the typewriter/word processor to enhance your display:
   - Consider the double spacing of capital letters for main titles:

     O P E R A T I O N   B U L L D O G

     and, if possible, the 'bold' alternative:

     O P E R A T I O N   B U L L D O G
   - Use capitals for main section headings, etc:

     PROBABLE EFFECT ON PRODUCTION

     and, again, the 'bold' alternative:

     PROBABLE EFFECT ON PRODUCTION
   - Use initial capitals underscored for subheadings within a main section, etc:

<u>New Furniture Required</u>

or the simpler version:

<u>New furniture required</u>

- Use italics to emphasize appropriate pieces of text:

  . . . as outlined in *The Secrets of Successful Business Letters* (Clive Goodworth, Heinemann, 1986)

  or by underscoring:

  . . . those personnel <u>primarily</u> responsible . . .

- If the facility is available, *always* have the text of a report justified. Unjustified text is text with a ragged right-hand edge – and, in this day and age, it's pretty old-hat.

2   Double or '1½' spacing of text makes it much easier to read, especially when the subject matter is of a complex nature. Also, don't forget that the recipient of the report may well wish to make the odd annotation here and there, and it's a tedious business doing this with single-spaced text, as well you know.

3   Always allow adequate margins. If a report is to be stapled or bound in any way, a left-hand margin of 1½ in is advisable.

4   A common failing of business writers (and typists/word processor operators) is to overlook the importance of indentation. If you wish your display to be spot-on, follow the golden rule:

2   MAIN SECTION HEADING

Main section text

(a)   Subsection text

(i)   Subordinate point text

or, where it is necessary to use subheadings:

2   MAIN SECTION HEADING
|
Main section text
|
Subsection heading
|
(a)   Subsection text
(i)   Subordinate point text

5   Ah, yes, I've just remembered . . . At the risk of insulting you, reader, if you still have a dog-eared stock of quarto or foolscap paper lurking in the stationery store – well, whatever you do, DON'T utilize this outdated stuff for reports. Use standard A4 paper, and your efforts will look all the better for it.

Workbox Number 2 has now drawn nigh. You'll need your word processor, typewriter or, at the very least, pen and paper for this one – but NOT your secretary, OK?

Workbox 2

Have a shot at improving the format-cum-display of the following report:

REPORT BY I. PRATT, PRODUCTION MANAGER, ON THE PERFORMANCE OF THE 'ULTRA' CAR JACK Mk I.

12th June, 1989.

For the attention of: L. P. Jeffries, Managing Director.

In response to increasing complaints from customers concerning the 'Ultra' Car Jack Mk I, the Managing Director instructed the writer to investigate the performance of the jack and to make recommendations accordingly. The report was required by 14th June, 1989.

In order to establish the performance range of the jack the following investigatory procedures were adopted:

A normal production sample of the jack was used to facilitate a wheel-change on two vehicles; namely: a Metro Saloon owned by P. Jones, Production Foreman and a Ford Sierra Saloon owned by the writer. A third test, utilizing a Rolls Royce Silver Cloud owned by the Managing Director, had been planned, but this was subsequently abandoned.

Since it was regarded as important that the jack should be operated by a relatively unskilled person, the three tests were carried out by Peter Ward, a Works Trainee and relatively inexperienced motorist.

The current situation is that the 'Ultra' Car Jack is advertised as suitable for use on all makes and models of car. The instructions for its use are quite explicit and include a clearly worded warning that the jack should not be used on soft or uneven ground.

Test No 1 (Metro). Having correctly positioned and operated the jack, Peter then proceeded to loosen the wheel nuts, preparatory to removing the wheel from the vehicle. While thus engaged, he noticed that the jack was slowly retracting to its closed position; thus lowering the vehicle towards the ground. He immediately retightened one wheel nut, but was unable to retighten the remaining nuts before the vehicle came to rest at ground level. It was noted by the writer that the piston casing of the jack emitted an audible hissing noise while thus subsiding.

Test No 2 (Sierra). In view of the outcome of the previous test, blocks of wood were stationed under the Sierra as a safety measure before the jack was placed in position and raised. As soon as the equipment was elevated to its maximum height, there was a loud bang and the jack collapsed with some violence. As a consequence, the Sierra fell on to the wooden blocks, which then toppled over, allowing the vehicle to fall heavily to the ground.

Test No 3 (Rolls Royce). In view of the outcome of the two previous tests, the writer did not deem it advisable or expedient to proceed with this phase of the investigation, and it was therefore abandoned.

The principal conclusions drawn by the writer were as follows.

Observation of the tests which were carried out indicated that the 'Ultra' Car Jack Mk I was unsuitable for use on any car, being incapable of supporting the weight of even a very light vehicle such as the Metro.

A detailed inspection of the fragmented components of the jack revealed that the likely cause of its premature retraction was the collapse under pressure of the piston seal. This diagnosis was subsequently confirmed following extensive laboratory and bench testing of the item in question.

Continued sale of this jack as presently constructed would inevitably result in many further complaints and the almost certain involvement of the company in potentially damaging litigation.

The writer strongly recommends that urgent consideration be given to implementing the following measures. The 'Ultra' Car Jack Mk I should be withdrawn from sale and dealer stocks returned to the factory for modification. A suitably worded warning should be published in the national press, together with an offer of free rectification.

(Signed)

I. Pratt.
Production Manager.

Tutorial to Workbox 2

Plainly, in terms of format and display, there is no one 'correct' version of Pratt's report, but before I offer my choice for your consideration, I'd like you to glance back at the text – and if you haven't done so already, take note of the punctuation. Modern convention dictates that business writing be given a crisper, cleaner look by deleting what are now regarded as entirely superfluous punctuation marks; for example:

- *Titles/headings*   Do not use a full stop at the end of a title or heading.
- *Names*   Do not use full stops between initials.
- *Names and
  addresses*   Again no full stops between initials – and note that commas are not used at the end of each line of the name and address:

> Mr I Pratt
> Production Manager
> Clangers Ltd
> 12–24 Orchard Way
> Huntingdon
> Cambs PE99 5NN

- *Dates*   Note that full stops, commas and those abbreviations 'th', 'nd' and 'st' are not used:

> 12th June, 1989. → 12 June 1989

So, with these provisions in mind, here is my version of Pratt's report.

REPORT BY I PRATT, PRODUCTION MANAGER, ON THE PERFORMANCE OF THE 'ULTRA' CAR JACK Mk I

12 June 1989

For the attention of:

Mr L P Jeffries
Managing Director

1 TERMS OF REFERENCE

In response to increasing complaints from customers concerning the 'Ultra' Car Jack Mk I, the Managing Director instructed the writer to investigate the performance of the jack and to make recommendations accordingly. The report was required by 14 June 1989.

2 PROCEDURE

In order to establish the performance range of the jack the following investigatory procedures were adopted:

(a) a normal production sample of the jack was used to facilitate a wheel-change on two vehicles; namely: a Metro Saloon owned by P. Jones, Production Foreman and a Ford Sierra Saloon owned by the writer;

(b) a third test, utilizing a Rolls Royce Silver Cloud owned by the Managing Director, had been planned, but this was subsequently abandoned;

(c) since it was regarded as important that the jack should be operated by a relatively unskilled person, the three tests were carried out by Peter Ward, a Works Trainee and relatively inexperienced motorist.

3 CURRENT SITUATION

The 'Ultra' Car Jack is advertised as suitable for use on all makes and models of car. The instructions for its use are quite explicit and include a clearly worded warning that the jack should not be used on soft or uneven ground.

4 FINDINGS

(a) <u>Test No 1 (Metro)</u> Having correctly positioned and operated the jack, Peter then proceeded to loosen the wheel nuts, preparatory to removing the wheel from the vehicle. While thus engaged, he noticed that the jack was slowly retracting to its closed position; thus lowering the vehicle towards the ground. He immediately retightened one wheel nut, but was unable to retighten the remaining nuts before the vehicle came to rest at ground level. It was noted by the writer that the piston casing of the jack emitted an audible hissing noise while thus subsiding;

(b) <u>Test No 2 (Sierra)</u> In view of the outcome of the previous test, blocks of wood were stationed under the Sierra as a safety measure before the jack was placed in position and raised. As soon as the equipment was elevated to its maximum height, there was a loud bang and the jack collapsed with some violence. As a consequence, the Sierra fell on to the wooden blocks, which then toppled over, allowing the vehicle to fall heavily to the ground;

(c)   <u>Test No 3 (Rolls Royce)</u> In view of the outcome of the two previous tests, the writer did not deem it advisable or expedient to proceed with this phase of the investigation, and it was therefore abandoned;

(d)   a detailed inspection of the fragmented components of the jack revealed that the likely cause of its premature retraction was the collapse under pressure of the piston seal. This diagnosis was subsequently confirmed following extensive laboratory and bench testing of the item in question.

5   CONCLUSIONS

The principal conclusions drawn by the writer were as follows:

(a)   the 'Ultra' Car Jack Mk I was unsuitable for use on any car, being incapable of supporting the weight of even a very light vehicle such as the Metro;

(b)   continued sale of this jack as presently constructed would inevitably result in many further complaints and the almost certain involvement of the company in potentially damaging litigation.

6   RECOMMENDATIONS

The writer strongly recommends that urgent consideration be given to implementing the following measures:

(a)   the 'Ultra' Car Jack Mk I should be withdrawn from sale and dealer stocks returned to the factory for modification;

(b)   a suitably worded warning should be published in the national press, together with an offer of free rectification.

(Signed)

I Pratt
Production Manager

Remember that business of choice. So long as your version of Pratt's report follows the rules I've outlined – why, you're home and dry!

Two final points

- You will have noticed that dear old Pratt penned his report in impersonal language, referring to himself in the third person. This is standard procedure for all formal reports.
- In my version of the report, I have included a heading ('CURRENT SITUATION') which does not appear in the lists of principal components of reports within this chapter. This is quite in order. *Provided your reports are compiled along the general lines of these lists, the actual wording of headings is entirely up to you.*

3   Report titles, tables of contents and terms of reference

> When I can read my title clear
> To mansions in the skies,
> I bid farewell to every fear,
> And wipe my weeping eyes.
> Isaac Watts (1674–1748), Hymn

Part A – Titles

Stand by for a resounding piece of logic. Anyone who writes a report is, *per se*, an author. And, as an author, unless you're blessed with a singular flair for apt and succinct composition, you'll suffer (along with yours truly and umpteen other pen pushers) a distinct difficulty in selecting the 'right' title for that masterpiece of the moment. The gurus of the report writing world offer but one rule for your guidance – and, although it has to be obeyed, I'm afraid it offers very little in the way of practical help:

THE TITLE (OR, IN THE CASE OF A LONG
FORMAL REPORT, THE TITLE-PAGE) MUST
SHOW *WHAT THE REPORT IS ABOUT AND BY
WHOM IT HAS BEEN WRITTEN*

Having stated the obvious, we find ourselves still stuck firmly on the launch pad – fishing madly in the waters of inspiration for that apt and succinct wording . . .

All of which is really a preamble to my admission that the best I can do is to illustrate by means of a few examples the good and not-so-good features of title compilation. So here goes.

Example 1
Imagine that Bill Cropper, a sales manager, is asked to write a

lengthy formal report on the outcome of a training needs analysis within his department. If our hero fails to pay sufficient attention to the need for this title to be worded in concise terms, he might well come up with something along these lines:

REPORT BY BILL CROPPER, SALES MANAGER, ON
THE TRAINING NEEDS ANALYSIS OF THE SALES
DEPARTMENT STAFF CARRIED OUT BY HIM
DURING THE PERIOD 22 MAY TO 26 MAY 1989

Bearing in mind the need for concise formality, I hope you will agree that one improved version of this title would be:

REPORT BY W CROPPER, SALES MANAGER, ON
THE TRAINING NEEDS ANALYSIS OF THE SALES
DEPARTMENT STAFF IMPLEMENTED DURING
THE PERIOD 22–26 MAY 1989

Or, since the report is lengthy, Bill could resort to a separate title page bearing the following:

REPORT ON THE TRAINING NEEDS ANALYSIS OF
SALES DEPARTMENT STAFF IMPLEMENTED
DURING THE PERIOD 22–26 MAY 1989
by
William Cropper
Sales Manager

Example 2

Suppose that Mary Tudor, a personnel officer, is required to write a report on a particular industrial tribunal hearing – and, after a bit of thought, comes up with the title:

REPORT BY MARY TUDOR, PERSONNEL OFFICER,
ON THE INDUSTRIAL TRIBUNAL HEARING HELD
AT HOBSON STREET, CAMBRIDGE, ON 20 JUNE
1989

It's probably safe to say that any recipient of Mary's report would wish the title to disclose *the identity of the applicant*, rather than the full address of the tribunal concerned, say, as follows:

REPORT BY MARY TUDOR, PERSONNEL OFFICER,
ON THE INDUSTRIAL TRIBUNAL HEARING

'CARTER LTD v P DUNN' HELD AT CAMBRIDGE ON 20 JUNE 1989

Example 3
Next, suppose that Charlie Bloggs, a test pilot, is charged with the task of writing a technical report on, wait for it, his assessment of the efficiency of wing fences and vortex generators in smoothing out the boundary layer airflow over the wing upper surface of Aircraft Prototype No 812B, following a series of flight trials during March 1989. My point in choosing this pig's orphan of an example is to remind you that *subtitles* are a handy way out when dealing with such lengthy but essential gobbledegook:

FLIGHT TESTS – AIRCRAFT PROTOTYPE 812B MARCH 1989

REPORT ON THE EFFICIENCY OF WING FENCES AND VORTEX GENERATORS IN SMOOTHING OUT BOUNDARY LAYER AIRFLOW OVER WING UPPER SURFACE

by

C Bloggs
Test Pilot

So, to repeat the message, the choice of an apt and succinct title requires very careful thought – and, particularly in the case of a technical report, it may be a good idea to postpone the chore until after the thing has been written.

Workbox 3

Turn back to Workbox Number 1 on page 10 and take another look at that list of titles. Omitting 3 and 7, have a go at improving the wording in each case.

Having done that like the zealous reader you are, examine the three examples above, and give them the same treatment.

Incidentally, the workboxes in this chapter will be falling round your ears like April showers. Do the best you can with 'em – we'll have a combined tutorial at the end of the chapter.

Part B – Tables of contents

If it is to make any sense to the recipient, the longer, more complex formal report must include a table of contents in which the headings and subheadings of each section and appendices, if any, are clearly set out. Since page numbers are obviously required, and since these will be known only once the final draft has been produced, it is down to the secretary or whoever to make the necessary, last-minute amendments to the list supplied by the writer. Figure 7 depicts a typical table of contents – note the format and display, and the use of '000' to signify where page numbers are required to be entered.

CONTENTS

		Page
1	Summary	0
2	Terms of reference	00
3	Introduction	00
4	Procedure	00
	4.1 Scope of the investigation	00
	4.2 Schedule of interviews	00
5	Interview reports	00
	5.1 S R Roberts	00
	5.2 Mrs V Williams	00
	5.3 T H Hubbard	00
6	Findings	000
	6.1 The current system	000
	6.2 Determination of loss	000
7	Conclusions	000
	7.1 Allocation of blame	000
8	Recommendations	000
Appendix 'A' – Photostat copy of Petty Cash Account Folio 25		000
Appendix 'B' – Photostat copy of Petty Cash Receipt No		000

Figure 7   A typical table of contents

Note that while a table of contents should have exactly the same wording where applicable as the headings in the text of the report, the amount of additional detail to be inserted is a matter of personal choice. But do remember that the object of the thing is to help the reader find a way through the jungle of text, not to render the poor creature a shivering mass of frustration.

Workbox 4

It is at this point that you have to start burrowing in the files. What I'd like you to do is to fish out the longest report you can lay your hands on – preferably one written by someone else. Then, assuming that it contains a table of contents, examine this with a critical eye and come up with a vastly improved version. If, perchance, the writer did not think fit to include a table of contents, you're jolly well not off the hook – gird your composition loins and produce one.

What's that I hear, grumpy muttering about it being a waste of valuable time? Well, we'll have less of that, my heartie – after all, you're the one who volunteered, so just get down to it, eh?

Part C – Terms of reference

In this guy's humble experience, many managers have more trouble with terms of reference than any other aspect of the report writing task. In fact, to be frank (and you wouldn't want me to be less than frank, would you?), there's a goodly number in our midst who are more than a little uncertain of the actual meaning of terms of reference – so let's scotch that one right away.

To put it somewhat crudely:

THE BUSINESS OF DECIDING EXACTLY
WHAT A REPORT IS ALL ABOUT
is
DEFINING YOUR TERMS OF REFERENCE

Sadly, with the possible exception of those who work in government departments, it seldom happens that the person who calls for a report will spell out concise terms of reference. More often than not, the hapless writer is kicked into perilous orbit by some such pearl as:

> Ah, Charles, about that missing equipment . . . Get something down on paper, there's a good chap . . . You know the sort of thing that's required – a full report of all the circumstances and what-not . . . Have it on my desk by Friday, will you?

So, for Charlie's sake alone (and he's not), it behoves us to examine the formulation of terms of reference in a bit more detail.

Terms of reference (ToR) authorize the writer★ to:

- investigate a given matter or situation for a specified purpose;
- conduct the investigation, call it what you will, within certain stated parameters;
- and, although this may not appear in the ToR as written down, formulate considered conclusions and recommendations.

Since I'm sure you will agree that the 'belt and braces' approach is vital when writing a report of any importance, I'd recommend that you include your authority for preparing it somewhere within the ToR.

Let's now take a look at some examples of ToR as they might appear in their respective report formats.

★ Note those words 'authorize the writer'. When you next require your junior to produce a report, ensure that you delegate the task wisely and well by providing adequate authority for the job to be done, i.e. by supplying concise ToR.

✕ 2　TERMS OF REFERENCE

The terms of reference authorized by the Managing Director for this report were as follows:

2.1　To investigate the current delays in production of Humiversal Filter pack-ups.

2.2　To examine alternative methods of overcoming the delays.

2.3　To make recommendations, accordingly.

1　TERMS OF REFERENCE

On 23 May 1989, the General Manager requested the members of the Works Council to investigate the services provided by the Works Canteen, report on their findings and make any necessary recommendations.

CAVIL & CARP LTD
Plumbers
55 The Marshes
Dampem Fen
Cambs PE85 9NN
Tel: 0488–978654

Mr R B Prickwillow　　　　　　　　　　14 June 1989
13 The Inundations
Outback
Cambs PE85 3FG

Dear Mr Prickwillow

Mains Water Supply

You instructed me on 9 June 1989 to investigate the possibility of obtaining a mains water connection to your bungalow, and authorized me to consult with Anglia Water on your behalf. I have now discussed the matter with their Area Engineer and

A word of warning

To some ego-impelled folk, the task of writing a report presents a heaven-sent opportunity to demonstrate what they fondly regard as their spare-no-punches, forthright manner – and, bingo, blinded by the brilliance of their own virtuosity, they drive a horse and cart straight through their respective ToR. Take my word for it, I've seen more than a few managers who've ended up thus hoisted by their own petards – and it's not a pretty sight.

Having said that, I reckon it's almost inevitable that, from time to time, you'll encounter situations in which it is absolutely necessary to step outside your allotted ToR, for the simple reason that the report won't make sense unless you do. This is fair enough, *provided* you say so; for example:

> Although it was not within the terms of reference of this investigation to examine . . ., the Working Party deemed it vital to the successful outcome of the inquiry to . . .

Workbox 5

1 Think of a suitable 'burning issue' at your place of work which, if only for the purpose of this paper exercise, merits detailed investigation and subsequent report. Now, come on, it can be anything under the sun; a problem concerning organization, production, communication, morale, car parking – or what have you. Having selected your subject, try your hand at writing the necessary ToR.
   IMPORTANT NOTE It is absolutely essential that you don't chicken out of this exercise – because, as you'll soon find out, your considered ToR are going to be the vehicle for your continued progression through a number of workboxes yet to come. A nod's as good as a wink!

2 If possible, think of an apt and succinct title for the report required in Task (1) – which, surprise, surprise, I am asking YOU to produce as you progress through this book.

As stated earlier, you'll find a combined tutorial at the end of this chapter.

CONFIDENTIAL

PERS/35/1/12/C

**PROGRESS REPORT ON THE
INTRODUCTION OF THE
PRIVATE MEDICAL SCHEME**

by

G B Simonds
Personnel Manager

For the attention of: 19 June 1989

Mr A R Wilberforce
Managing Director

CONFIDENTIAL

Figure 8(a)   Part of a typical formal report – depicting, in conjunction
with Figures 8(b) and 8(c), the components covered thus far

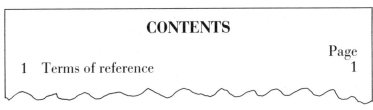

CONTENTS

                                                    Page
1   Terms of reference   1

Figure 8(b)   Part of a typical formal report – depicting, in conjunction
with Figures 8(a) and 8(c), the components covered thus far

– 1 –

1   TERMS OF REFERENCE
    The writer was instructed by the Managing Director to
    investigate the degree of overall success of the newly-
    implemented private medical scheme and to make
    recommendations, accordingly.

Figure 8(c)   Part of a typical formal report – depicting, in conjunction
with Figures 8(a) and 8(b), the components covered thus far

And now for the big yin . . .

It's at this juncture that I'd like to introduce you to the first
chunk of what I choose to call an 'ongoing example' of report
writing. Figure 8 comprises the title, table of contents and
terms of reference of a typical formal investigation report. In
successive chapters, as we plod through the other component
parts of a report, the ongoing example will 'build up' in
relevant stages – to the point at which the complete document
is portrayed. So, in a sense, we're going to be working in
harness – you with your report, and me with mine.

I suppose that's just about as far as we can get in achieving a
'combined effort' – so good luck.

Tutorial to Workboxes 3, 4 and 5

Since I'm a bit short on the old sixth sense, I have no idea what you've come up with in response to these workboxes – so I'm not in a very good position to make comment. However, the main thing is, you've done what you were asked, haven't you? Well, *haven't* you?

If, as I surmise, you really wish to improve your report writing skills (for why else are you ploughing through this book?), there is but one way to bring this about – and the name of the game is PRACTICE. It is for this reason that I've clobbered you with the task of writing a full report – which, as I've already indicated, is best achieved by doing a chunk at a time, keeping pace with successive chapters.

Assuming that you're a glutton for punishment, here's a final note on cooking up terms of reference. They must not be too vague. So, on the one hand, if you're ever served up with inexplicit ToR tell whoever is responsible – very politely, mind – that they just won't suffice. On the other hand, if *you* are delegating the job of writing a report, however minor, to some other hapless soul, make quite certain that your ToR are pearls of breadth and accuracy.

4 Report summaries and introductions

Enough! I would but taste the flavour.
  For, cry as you will,
I may not like the dish.

Anon.

Summaries

Of all the resources available to managers in their work, only one is truly finite – and that is time. It is therefore tragically ironic that, while we at least endeavour to manage the classic three Ms,* we pay scant attention indeed to that age-old but eminently relevant caveat:

Sed fugit interea, fugit inreparabile tempus

or, if like me, you didn't take Latin at school:

Meanwhile time is flying, flying never to return

Our arrant disregard for efficient time management was bad enough in the old days; but today, whether we like it not, we're being well-nigh swept off our executive feet by an incredible communications revolution – and if we're to survive we *must* use time to our advantage in coping with this hydra of the technological age in which we live.

If practised effectively, the art of summarising can be of tremendous help in our continuing dilemma of having too much to do in too little time. Unfortunately, as some of us will remember from those précis-ridden English lessons at school, it's like any other art – a few have the gift, but most of us are

---

* No, officially not Morons, Mess-ups and Mistakes, but Men, Money and Materials.

daubers, needing constant practice and guidance if we're to achieve even fair results. That being so, I'll flash a quick definition of a report summary in front of your eyes, and then try to give you some help.

> **The object of a report summary is to enable the reader to get a swift gist of what the report is about and, in particular, an indication of the conclusions drawn and the recommendations arising from them.**

Coping with report summaries

Since we're all good trainers at heart (!!), let's start by pinpointing the component skills which make up the art of summarizing – be it reports we're concerned with, or anything else.

Comprehension	This is the ability to understand a chunk of information, data or opinion – and, just as important, the ability to infer meaning from it.
Classification	This is the ability to put one's finger fairly and squarely on salient points for a particular purpose.
Analysis	In monkey-talk, the ability to be a nitpicker, or, if you prefer it, to pick out the wheat from the chaff – in other words, the skill of sifting and evaluating material in order to distinguish the essential from the inessential.
Evaluation	The ability to weigh information and data – and, if it is a heaven-sent ability, to weigh opinion.
Selection	The ability to sift further – finally to select the salient points/issues for use in the summary.
Objectivity	The key ability to work in such a manner that personal opinion and bias do not intrude upon, or infect, one's efforts.
Composition	A poor term for a vital component – skill with words, such that the sum-

mary will faithfully reflect the facts, tone and/or attitudes of the original material.

A pretty daunting list of abilities, methinks – and I'm afraid I have to make things more daunting still by adding that a fall-down in just one of the component areas will virtually guarantee a poor summary.

Having cast gloom and doom withal, I'd better give that promised help – so here goes with a checklist for your considered digestion.

A checklist for compiling report summaries

It follows as the night the day that you cannot attempt to summarize that which you haven't written – so, ramming home the obvious in painful fashion, compiling the summary is probably your penultimate report writing task. Penultimate, because in all likelihood, there's the small matter of that table of contents. Now to the checklist.

1 Read the report through quickly in order to grasp the general sense (or nonsense . . .) of the thing. If it's a long and complex document, there's no escape – it's your dearly-loved baby, but several rereads may be necessary. Cruel comment or not, it's at this first step in the checklist that most *rewrites* are spawned.
2 Read the report thoroughly, section by section, noting the division of subject matter, and the relative importance you have attached to each such division.
3 List the key topics.
4 From the list, compose a rough draft of the summary – ensuring that, instead of taking the fatal way out and merely copying bits from the original, you resort to new wording. It stands to reason that if you don't do this, you won't end up with a true summary – but, rather, a pure and simple botch-up.
5 Now comes the tough bit. Check and edit the rough draft mercilessly to ensure that it reads smoothly, logically and intelligibly.
6 Even tougher . . . Check the final draft against the full report to ensure that it is, in fact, a comprehensive summary. If it isn't, go back to Number 1 and start again.

ACCIDENT TO COMPANY VEHICLE F878TRG

	Primary Importance	Secondary Importance	Minor Importance
1	Company driver's statement – BH Browne		
2	Eye-witness report – Miss A Plumb		
3		Eye-witness report – H Williams	
4		Photographs of scene taken following day, when road dry	
5			Eye-witness report – child cyclist John Middleton
6	Cpy insurance accident claim		
7	Report on damage to vehicle – D Roberts Ltd		
8	Estimate for repairs – D Roberts Ltd (£545.75)		
9		Estimate for repairs – Whyte Autos Ltd (£710.50)	
10			Estimate for repairs – Star Garage (£733.60)

Figure 9   A typical example of a 'pre-report summary' showing sequential arrangement of material, and the degree of importance attached to each item

7 Ask yourself the sixty thousand dollar one: are you absolutely certain that the recipient will clearly understand what you've written – and that, after the full report has been read, it will be pronounced a good summary?

If you're really seeking to improve your summarizing skills, there's only one way to go about it – and that is to practise, and practise hard. I now intend to give you a friendly kick in the right direction with the next workbox.

Workbox 6

1 Applying the checklist, summarize the following passage. There is no need to quote the source of the material.

> On the Japanese left General Oku advanced to the neighbourhood of Kaiping early in July, in the face of heavy rains. The Russians had counted on their enemy being greatly delayed by the bad weather, and were taken by surprise by the rapid Japanese forward movement. For strategic reasons it was impossible for them as yet to abandon the town of Kaiping, and General Sampsonoff received orders to hold it with a division of Cossacks, supported by a small detachment of infantry, so as to impede the Japanese march northward as far as possible and give General Stakelberg time to withdraw the shaken remnant of his army, which was not as yet in a condition to face the victorious Japanese. The Russians occupied a line of positions on the heights immediately to the east of Kaiping, running generally parallel to the railway, and were threatened not only with a frontal attack by General Oku's army, but also with envelopment by General Nodzu's force, which made demonstrations against their rear, advancing westwards from the Shapanling Pass and the neighbourhood of Hsiahata. The Russian position was thus an insecure one, and all idea of a determined resistance at this point had to be abandoned.
>
> *Japan's Fight for Freedom (The Russo-Japanese War)*
> H. W. Wilson, 1905

2 And, bless'ee, do the same again.

   All forms of private enterprise and public works must be scrutinised. We must ask the question: 'Are they diverting labour and energies which should be devoted to the defence of Britain?'

   If you walk through the streets of our cities you can see builders and concrete mixers working on new buildings and offices. Not one of these men should be put out of work. Nothing is gained by swelling the numbers on the unemployment register. But some builders could be transferred to jobs of more urgent importance. Their skill and their materials could be used to make modern Martello towers.

   When Napoleon threatened the invasion of England, Martello towers were built round the coast. Today our Martello towers must be all over the country. Anti-aircraft batteries, air-raid shelters, sandbags and fortified posts guarding every important building.

   If you walk through the country, you can see ducal parks and golf courses. They are green and pleasant and completely useless. Worse. They are a danger. Every smooth lawn, every fairway, could be a landing ground for transport planes carrying German troops. They should be ploughed up now and cleaned ready for autumn cropping. One way to guard against invasion is to plough and plant each expanse of flat ground.

   Daily Express, Editorial
   31 May 1940

3 Lest you've indulged in a wee moan over the fact that the two preceding tasks have nothing to do with business (which is quite deliberate, since it does us all good to get away from the office now and again), here's a 'work-oriented' example for your delight. Summarize, please.

R&D/23/2/86

CONFIDENTIAL

CDA COMPUTERS LTD

PROTOTYPE MODEL X34
SPECIFICATION OF REQUIREMENTS

1 Introduction

Prototype Model X34 reflects the company's decision to achieve market penetration in the field of low-priced, user-friendly text editing equipment.

2 Function

  2.1 When used in conjunction with the CDA Electronic Typewriter or other suitably interfaced equipment, which will double as operating keyboard and printer, the X34 is required to provide an eminently user-friendly text-editing facility. The X34 will be a screen-based system with limited document, phrase and format memories, and is intended to offer a fully comprehensive range of text editing activities by means of simple menu instruction.

  2.2 The system is required to offer subsequent optional connection to a conventional audio-cassette recorder, to enable single documents or selected memory contents to be stored on a conventional music cassette.

3 Components

The X34 is required to comprise;

  (a) a central processing system containing an integrated 32K universal memory with an available capacity of 29,600 characters, extendable by 2 × 16,400 characters, thereby providing a maximum capacity of 62,400 characters of available memory;

  (b) a typewriter interface;

  (c) a display screen with 58 lines, each line with 80 characters, in black on white background.

4 Additional requirements

  4.1 (a) *CPU* To be micro-processor-controlled,

with a three-month data retention capability. The CPU is required to be housed in a flat container capable of use as a mounting base for the screen unit, and is to be provided with a suitable turntable for this purpose:

(i)   Maximum permissible dimensions: 80 mm (height) × 400 mm (width) × 280 mm (depth).

(ii) Maximum permissible weight: 2.5 kg.

(iii) power supply: 220-240 volts, 50-60 Hz.

(b) *Screen* To be rectangular to suit required lineage, and of minimum height commensurate with the design. The screen base to be provided with a connecting plate designed to mate with the turntable on the CPU. Further criteria are as follows:

(i)   other maximum permissible dimensions: 380 mm (width) × 340 mm (depth);

(ii) maximum permissible weight: 7 kg;

(iii) power supply: 220–240 volts, 50–60 Hz.

5   Reference

For material specifications and basic construction criteria, refer to CDA Project Specification R&D/26/2/85 dated 9 July 1985.

C R Roberts
R & D Manager   19 April 1986

The Secrets of Successful Business Letters,
Clive Goodworth, Heinemann 1986

Introductions

When compiling a lengthy and/or complex report, it is imperative that one includes an introductory section. This should set out:

1 Sufficient background information to put the recipient in the general picture.
2 The reason(s) the report has been called for.
3 An indication of the area(s) to be covered.
4 Ideally, an explanation of how the report subject is to be developed.

Obviously, the actual wording of report introductions will vary enormously, but if you follow the above guidelines, you'll be well on track to success.

Workbox 7

It's time for your second dig in those filing cabinets . . . Seek out a goodly number of reports and divide 'em into two piles – those with introductions and those without. First, inspect the existing introductions with a critical eye and ask yourself, do they fulfil their respective purposes in every respect – and if not, why? Second, pick out one of the longer reports which lacks an introduction – and, yes, compile one.

More on the big yin

We now come to Figure 10, the second stage of our brick-by-brick, ongoing example of a typical report, which will bring us up to date where this chapter is concerned. And, don't forget, you are supposed to be putting in further practice by writing *your* report!

Tutorial to Workboxes 6 and 7

Workbox 6

I imagine that you've undergone a spot of frustration in trying to decide *how long* your summaries should be. Well, bearing in mind that one seldom, if ever, receives instructions on this point when charged with the task of writing a real-life report, the only rules of thumb I can offer are as follows:
1 Refrain from any thought of length until such time as the

<u>**CONFIDENTIAL**</u>

PERS/35/1/12/C

**PROGRESS REPORT ON THE
INTRODUCTION OF THE
PRIVATE MEDICAL SCHEME**

by

G B Simonds
Personnel Manager

For the attention of: 19 June 1989

    Mr A R Wilberforce
    Managing Director

<u>**CONFIDENTIAL**</u>

Figure 10(a)   Part of a typical formal report – depicting, in conjunction with Figures 10(b) and 10(c), the components covered thus far

---

CONTENTS

Figure 10(b)   Part of a typical formal report – depicting, in conjunction with Figures 10(a) and 10(c), the components covered thus far

rough draft (stage 5 of the checklist in this chapter) has been completed.

2   Check throughout the draft for points which, albeit are perhaps relevant, are *not essential*. Be merciless and prune them out.

3   Lastly, cast a very critical eye over the actual wording of the remaining text. Examine each and every word for its contribution to the whole – and, once again, wield that pruning knife. Make one word do the work of two, and so on.

Task 1

Here is an effort at summarizing this rather knotty piece on the Russo-Japanese War. Note the words underlined in the initial rough draft, which to my mind are relevant but not essential.

In early [DELETE] July, despite the [DELETE] bad weather, the Japanese General Oku carried out a surprise advance [SUBSTITUTE advanced suddenly/unexpectedly] to the Russian-held Kaiping area. Obliged strategically [DELETE] to hold the town of Kaiping, General Samsonoff's Cossacks, aided by some [DELETE] infantry, strove to impede the Japanese advance northward [DELETE] and thus allow General Stakelberg's depleted, war-weary [SUBSTITUTE exhausted] troops to withdraw. The Russian positions east of Kaiping [SUBSTITUTE Russians] were threatened not only [DELETE] with Oku's frontal assault, but also with an attack from their rear [SUBSTITUTE and also with a rear attack] by General Nodzu's force, [SUBSTITUTE Nodzu] advancing westwards [DELETE] from the Shapanling Pass and Hsiahata. Their insecurity thus precluded any thought of [DELETE] determined resistance.

– 1 –

1   TERMS OF REFERENCE
The writer was instructed by the Managing Director to investigate the degree of overall success of the newly-implemented private medical scheme and to make recommendations, accordingly.

2   SUMMARY
(a)   Subject of the report   This report details the implementation and findings of a survey carried out by the writer to determine the extent to which voluntary membership of the private medical scheme had been taken up by employees and, *inter alia*, to assess the overall success or otherwise of the scheme.
(b)   Conclusions   It was concluded that since, as revealed by the survey, some 92% of those eligible had opted for membership and the Privamed Society had already actioned a significant number of claims, the scheme was operating successfully. As a result of widespread enquiries made during the survey, it was further concluded that the scheme was generally regarded as an important and much-appreciated employee benefit.
(c)   Recommendations   The writer recommends that the scheme be continued as presently constituted, and that eligible employees who have not already opted for membership should be individually counselled in relation to the many advantages offered by cost-free medical insurance.

Figure 10(c)   Part of a typical formal report – depicting, in conjunction with Figures 10(a) and 10(b), the components covered thus far

Report summaries and introductions 57

– 2 –

3 INTRODUCTION
The private medical scheme, offering a wide range of free
medical insurance benefits to all employees with over
twelve months' continuous service, was introduced on 1
March 1989. Notwithstanding that the scheme enjoyed
swift and general popularity, it was considered desirable
that a survey be conducted in order to assess the degree of
this success in more precise terms, and make recommendations accordingly. Tasked with this survey, the
writer decided that it would be best achieved by a three-
fold approach:
(a) an examination of the available statistics on
membership numbers and claims made during the
first three months' operation of the scheme;
(b) a series of interviews conducted with the aim of
seeking the views of a representative sample of those
employees who had enrolled for membership;
(c) a series of interviews conducted with the aim of
seeking the views of a representative sample of those
employees who had declined membership of the
scheme.

Figure 10(c) *(Continued)*

By actioning these amendments, we are left with a final draft,
as follows:

In July, despite bad weather, the Japanese General Oku
advanced suddenly to the Russian-held Kaiping area. Obliged
to hold the town of Kaiping, General Samsonoff's Cossacks,
aided by infantry, strove to impede the Japanese advance and
thus allow General Stakelberg's exhausted troops to withdraw. The Russians were threatened with Oku's frontal assault
and also with a rear attack by General Nodzu, advancing from
the Shapanling Pass and Hsiahata. Their insecurity thus
precluded any determined resistance.

Now, one man's meat can certainly be another man's poison,
and it may well be that, given the choice, you would prefer
something between the two versions illustrated above. On the
other hand, you may entertain a definite preference for *your*

beautifully executed final draft! The main thing is, have I got you thinking?

Task 2
Here's a final draft summary of the piece of editorial. See how you can improve it; and, of course, compare it with your own.

> The question of diverting construction workers to more pressing wartime tasks must be considered. Their skills could be utilized to make the air-raid shelters and other fortifications which, like the Martello towers of old, should be strategically positioned throughout Britain. The country abounds in areas of smooth, flat grassland, which offer ready-made landing facilities for German troop-carriers. One way to guard against invasion is to plough and plant each such dangerous expanse.

Task 3
And, finally, here is a summary of the specification of requirements for your similar consideration.

Summary
This specification details the basic components and associated design criteria for the projected X34 text editor.

And it's as simple as that – mainly for the reason that such a short document really does not warrant a summary.

Hey-ho, we're getting on. The next chapter's a fairly meaty one, so this might be a good point at which to pour a stiff noggin and take a well-earned break from your labours. Prost!

5   Coping with the body of a report

So, in this way of writing without thinking,
Thou hast a strange alacrity in sinking.
Thomas Sackville, Earl of Dorset (1536–1608)
Satire on Edward Howard

At long last, we come to the nub of the matter, the quintessence of our study, coping with the main body of a report. Y'know, if there was a graveyard reserved exclusively for managers (now there's a thought), there's little doubt that many of the tombstones would bear some grim and telling epitaphs, like:

ERECTED TO THE MEMORY OF CHAS.
ENTWHISTLE
MANAGER (FAILED)
Who wrote a report and, shortly thereafter,
was despatched from this world by
a quick bullet
He paid the price for finding out,
Nor never grudged the price he paid,
But nestles here without his boots,
Marvelling at the mess he made.

You think I'm joking? Well, you just think on't. A formal report to the boss, or anyone else for that matter, is probably the most formidable piece of writing yer average manager will ever be called upon to churn out. And, terrible prospect, if Big Daddy Gradgrind has a sudden yen to see his minion's writing warts displayed in all their horrible glory, there's no better way than to task the poor wretch with producing a formal report. For this and umpteen other reasons, I'm going to kick off this chapter by inviting you to take an inquisitive sniff at some of the major difficulties of the game.

But first I'd better mention the obvious, namely that much

of what follows is applicable to report writing in general, and not just to the main body of a report. If there's an excuse for this apparent departure from my chosen format, it's merely that I wish to avoid needless repetition throughout the book, OK? Right, now we'll press on.

The body of the report

Plainly, the body of the report (sometimes referred to as the 'procedure' because it deals with the methods used to collect data or information, tests carried out, etc.) is the proverbial meat in the sandwich. The foremost rule to bear in mind is that the body of any report must consist of *facts*, and *nothing else*; in other words, *what actually was* and *what is*.

There is absolutely no place in this impartial exposition of facts for personal opinions, inferences or prejudices. So far as the writer's personal views and deductions are concerned, and always provided they are relevant to the subject under report, these will come later in the report. As for prejudices – well, I think we can take it as read that no report writer worth his salt would dream of being other than totally impartial throughout the work.

Let me ram that vital point home:

THE BODY	››	FACTS AND	››	WHAT ACTUALLY
OF THE	››	NOTHING	››	WAS AND WHAT
REPORT	››	ELSE	››	IS

Gathering the data

Having identified the purpose and scope of the report (those terms of reference, remember?), it is down to the writer to decide exactly how the data, *all* the data, is to be gathered:

BY INTERVIEWING PEOPLE
BY SCRUTINIZING PAPERWORK
BY OBSERVING OPERATIONS/PROCEDURES, ETC
BY INSPECTING SITES, ETC

and vital to each of the above:

BY EXAMINATION AND ANALYSIS OF THE REVEALED FACTS AND DATA

Interviewing people

While the vexed subject of interviewing, *per se*, is outside the scope of this book, perhaps you'll forgive me if I remind you about the invaluable 'Magic Six' rule. When interviewing for the purpose of factfinding, ask as many open-ended questions as possible, prefacing each with one of the Magic Six:

> HOW. . . ?
> WHY. . . ?
> WHAT. . . ?
> WHEN. . . ?
> WHICH. . . ?
> WHO. . . ?

The requirement that the writer must present an impersonal, factual account within the body of the report does not mean that, during the investigative stage, the views and prejudices of others should also be regarded as forbidden fruit. Far from it. If Manager X expresses a view, this should be reported as such *precisely*, for this is the very stuff of factual reporting.

Scrutinizing paperwork

Thankfully, in the majority of cases, getting one's hands on the paperwork essential to a report writing task is pretty straightforward. However, Sod's Law ensures that there'll come a time when, for some nefarious reason or other, part or even all of it, will have vanished into thin air. In such instances, *never* succumb to the temptation of saying to yourself, 'Ah well, not to worry – I can get by,' or some such similar cop-out. There is a very good reason for warning you thus, because Sod's Law may well dictate that, once a report has been rendered and it's too gosh-darned late to retrieve it, the missing paperwork will suddenly turn up – and then, my friend, you'll be up that odorous, over-crowded creek without a vestige of a paddle.

Remember, too, that paperwork breeds paperwork. Check on the circulation route and addressee(s) of each document, making absolutely certain that you get your acquisitive fingers on anything that might have the slightest bearing on the task.

Observing operations/procedures, etc.
It's just not sufficient to stand and gawp – and, having gawped, wander back to one's desk with a batch of memories and impressions. If you or your outfit can't afford one of those excellent pocket recorders with which to immortalize your on-the-spot observations, then, for goodness sake, arm yourself with a clipboard – or, if the cap fits, a slate. And what about a camera?

Inspecting sites, etc.
Obviously, when faced with compiling an investigative report (say, for example, an accident report), it is absolutely essential to inspect the site concerned with a minimum of delay. In such instances, the following action checklist may be helpful:

1　Ensure adequate photographic coverage of the site, as found.
2　Draw an exact scaled plan of the area, depicting all relevant detail.
3　Establish, by recourse to eye-witnesses and any physical evidence, the extent and nature of any changes/removals which have taken place since the incident occurred. Record the necessary detail photographically, in note form and on the plan.
4　In the case of accidents or other such significant events, procure written statements from all those interviewed, and check each person's future availability in the event that further interviewing will be required.

Organizing the data

Having accumulated the relevant data, the report writer is then faced with the task of organizing it into a coherent, usable and relevant form.

Step 1   Assemble the data in chronological or other suitable
         sequence.
Step 2   Decide which facts are of primary importance, secon-
         dary importance and so on. It's at this stage that the
         eyes should be kept peeled for any anomalies in the
         data; for example, indications that, as currently
         amassed, the facts do not present a complete picture
         and that further investigation is necessary.
Step 3   It will often be helpful to produce a summary of the
         action taken in Steps 1 and 2. Take a glance at Figure
         9, which depicts just such a summary.

Producing the body of the report

Having organized the data in terms of sequential order and
degrees of importance, the inexperienced report writer could
be forgiven for thinking that all that remains is to plunge into
glorious composition. But, in all save the most straightforward of issues, this would be courting disaster – for it is at this
stage that the mind must turn to the all-important question of
the *final review*.

A checklist for conducting the final review

1   Albeit that the data has been organized as above, are there
    significant facts buried within the clumps of material
    which have a bearing on one another?
2   Do any of the facts contradict one another?
3   Are there any irrelevancies for rejection?
4   And, once again, are there gaps in the data which need to
    be explored and rectified?

It is only when this final sifting, analysing and, perhaps,
reorganization of the data has been completed that the writer
can safely embark on compiling the various clearly defined
sections which, in sum, will comprise the body of the report.

Workbox 8

Again, grab hold of some of those filed reports and, adopting your most critical stance, inspect their respective bodies. I would like you to look for:

- evidence that the writers have expressed their own views or, worse, reflected prejudice therein;
- apparent irrelevancies in the texts;
- ill-organized presentation in terms of the component sections (or lack of them);
- general lack of clarity, with an accent on ambiguity;
- the writer's use of needless jargon and commercialese.

Exercise your mind, prith'ee, by determining (in rough note form) how you would rectify the deficiencies you find.

And so to the big yin

Although you should be getting used to the procedure by now, let me just remind you that Figure 11 depicts the third stage of our brick-by-brick, ongoing example of a typical report. As you will see, it now includes a body (that's an odd way of putting it, and no mistake) and, being the keen type you are, you're going to cast a hypercritical eye over the thing, aren't you?

And, of course, look carefully at *your* ongoing masterpiece!

A few of the pitfalls

Formality

Up to the present, I've used the term 'formal report' with something approaching gay abandon and, although we've dealt with the business of formality in format and display, we haven't even touched on the most important and knottiest aspect of all, formality of style.

<u>**CONFIDENTIAL**</u>

PERS/35/1/12/C

**PROGRESS REPORT ON THE
INTRODUCTION OF THE
PRIVATE MEDICAL SCHEME**

by

G B Simonds
Personnel Manager

For the attention of: 19 June 1989

    Mr A R Wilberforce
    Managing Director

<u>**CONFIDENTIAL**</u>

Figure 11(a)   Part of a typical formal report – depicting, in conjunction with Figures 11(b) and 11(c), the components covered thus far

CONTENTS

		Page
1	Terms of reference	1
2	Summary	1
3	Introduction	2
4	Findings	3

Figure 11(b)   Part of a typical formal report – depicting, in conjunction with Figures 11(a) and 11(c), the components covered thus far

One inescapable convention employed in the writing of all but the most informal of reports is the use of what the gurus describe as *impersonal construction*. This simply means that one avoids like the plague using those pleasant little first person pronouns, 'I', 'me', 'we' and 'us', and so on – and instead uses much stodgier forms:

(a) Use by the author of the third person to refer to him/herself

>NOT   'I interviewed the manager concerned . . .'
>BUT   'The writer interviewed the manager concerned . . .'
>OR   'The General Manager interviewed the manager concerned . . .' (when the writer *is* the General Manager).

>NOT   'In my view, this was irregular . . .'
>BUT   'In the writer's view, this was irregular . . .'
>OR   'In the Controller's view, this was irregular . . .' (when the writer *is* the Controller).

(b) Use of passive impersonal constructions
>'The suspect was then arrested and charged with . . .'
>'It was subsequently found that . . .'

One massive disadvantage of such formality is that it's pretty cold stuff and, as a consequence, entirely devoid of all the niceties that can, and always should, characterize other forms of person-to-person communication in business. But, like it

– 1 –

1   TERMS OF REFERENCE
The writer was instructed by the Managing Director to investigate the degree of overall success of the newly-implemented private medical scheme and to make recommendations, accordingly.

2   SUMMARY
(a)   Subject of the report   This report details the implementation and findings of a survey carried out by the writer to determine the extent to which voluntary membership of the private medical scheme had been taken up by employees and, *inter alia*, to assess the overall success or otherwise of the scheme.

(b)   Conclusions   It was concluded that since, as revealed by the survey, some 92% of those eligible had opted for membership and the Privamed Society had already actioned a significant number of claims, the scheme was operating successfully. As a result of widespread enquiries made during the survey, it was further concluded that the scheme was generally regarded as an important and much-appreciated employee benefit.

(c)   Recommendations   The writer recommends that the scheme be continued as presently constituted, and that eligible employees who have not already opted for membership should be individually counselled in relation to the many advantages offered by cost-free medical insurance.

Figure 11(c)   Part of a typical formal report – depicting, in conjunction with Figures 11(a) and 11(b), the components covered thus far

– 2 –

3   INTRODUCTION
The private medical scheme, offering a wide range of free medical insurance benefits to all employees with over twelve months' continuous service, was introduced on 1 March 1989. Notwithstanding that the scheme enjoyed swift and general popularity, it was considered desirable that a survey be conducted in order to assess the degree of this success in more precise terms, and make recommendations accordingly. Tasked with this survey, the writer decided that it would be best achieved by a three-fold approach:

(a)   an examination of the available statistics on membership numbers and claims made during the first three months' operation of the scheme;

(b)   a series of interviews conducted with the aim of seeking the views of a representative sample of those employees who had enrolled for membership;

(c)   a series of interviews conducted with the aim of seeking the views of a representative sample of those employees who had declined membership of the scheme.

Figure 11(c)   *(continued)*

– 3 –

4 FINDINGS

A <u>Membership and Use of the Scheme</u>

(i) A survey of the personnel records revealed that, as at 14 July 1989, 564 employees had completed twelve months' continuous service with the company, and were therefore eligible to join the private medical scheme.

(ii) Of this number, 518 employees (91.8%) had enrolled in the scheme.

(iii) Figures produced by the Privamed Society (see Appendix) show that during the period 1 March to 14 July 1989, inclusive, a total of 53 claims were received from members, of which 48 had been settled and the remainder were awaiting payment. When the rate of claims, some 10.2%, was queried, Mr H T Heslop, the Privamed representative, stated his opinion that, in view of the prevailing weather during the period, the figure could rightly be regarded as 'low-average'.

B <u>Members' Views of the Scheme</u>

(i) In order to gain a more accurate indication of the popularity of the scheme, a total of 52 members (representing a cross-section of the company, and comprising 4 managers, 10 supervisors and 38 clerical staff) were interviewed by the writer and the Welfare Officer. Of those interviewed, a total of 26 members had submitted claims, all of which had been settled by Privamed.

Figure 11(c) *(continued)*

– 4 –

(ii)   While due allowance must be made for the subjective nature of the exercise, certain specific questions produced responses as shown:

(a)   To what extent are you satisfied with the benefits offered by the private medical scheme?

Very satisfied	Satisfied
21	27

Minimally satisfied	Dissatisfied
4	Nil

(b)   Now that you know the annual cost to the company of the scheme, do you think this money should have been expended on some other employee benefit?

No	Yes
51	1

(iii)   (c)   (Addressed to the 26 members who had submitted claims.) To what extent are you satisfied with Privamed's handling of your claim(s)?

Very satisfied	Satisfied
24	2

Figure 11(c)   *(continued)*

– 5 –

C   Views of employees who had declined member-
     ship
     (i)   In order to gain a more accurate indica-
           tion why 46 employees had declined
           membership of the scheme, all concerned
           were briefly interviewed by the writer and
           the Welfare Officer. Of this total, 11
           employees stated that they had changed
           their minds and wished to join the
           scheme. The necessary applications have
           been completed in respect of this group,
           with membership to commence w.e.f. 1
           August 1989.
     (ii) Of the remaining 35 employees, 23 gave
           as their reason for refusing membership
           the fact that they were opposed to the
           principle of private medical treatment on
           political grounds. In the case of the
           remaining 12 employees, it was not pos-
           sible to establish conclusive reasons for
           their rejection of the scheme, but there
           were indications that some individuals
           thought that, as private patients, they
           would be 'singled out' from those under-
           going National Health Service treatment;
           and, as a consequence, would feel embar-
           rassment and/or social unease. However,
           7 of the 12 did state that they would give
           the matter further consideration.

Figure 11(c)   *(continued)*

or not, we're stuck with the convention and there's no alternative but to grin and bear it.

Clarity

There are those among us who, by virtue of their jobs, are required to read reports day in and day out. Ask any number of these unenvied folk to pronounce on the frustrations inherent in such work, and it's odds-on that 'lack of clarity' will be at the top of their list. From my point of view, this is a devil, because there's no way that any reader who has difficulty in achieving clarity of writing is going to emerge from this book very much better at the art. Now, that's honest enough, isn't it?

What I can do is to offer some tips for clear writing, and urge that if this is one of your particular hang-ups, you take 'em well and truly to heart – and then get yourself enrolled on a suitable course. ★

Sentence construction
While it is a golden rule for easy reading that sentences should vary in structure and length, a second and important rule dictates that, on average, they should be short.

Choice of words
Since intelligence and size of vocabulary are closely linked, it is very easy for some worthies to use words that are as plain as piecrust to the writer – and utterly flummoxing to the reader. Contrary to what many executive bigheads believe, a report writing task does *not* carry an inbuilt licence to show off . . .

Unfortunately, many of us often *misuse words* because we do not understand their true meaning; for example:

*Accommodating three clerks in this office is not **practical**.*

The correct word is *practicable*.

★ In these enlightened days, one *pleasantly* effective way of improving one's writing skills is to undertake an open learning course. If the need is there, I strongly recommend that you contact your nearest open learning unit. Your local college should be able to steer you in the right direction.

*His performance was adversely **effected** by the conditions under which he was forced to work.*

The correct word is *affected*.

*He was **disinterested** in the work.*

The correct word is *uninterested*.

Ambiguity

(a) As with all other aspects of communication, the aim of the report writer must be to produce sentences *capable of one meaning only*. Consider the following horror:

> *The managing director informed Mr Phipps that he had been at fault.*

You tell me, is that ambiguity, or not? Now try this one for size:

> *Having returned to the office a fortnight later, he was suspended from work by his departmental manager, who informed him that he had been trying to rearrange the overtime roster.*

Well, who had? As I'm sure you'll appreciate, both of the above examples illustrate how the careless use of those insignificant little things *pronouns* can cause communicational havoc.

(b) Similarly, the correct positioning of *adverbs* within a sentence is crucial; for example:

> *That manager **only** was familiar with the procedure.*

He didn't know a great deal about the procedure?

> *That manager was familiar **only** with the procedure.*

And nothing else?

> ***Only** that manager was familiar with the procedure.*

No one else knew anything about it?

Jargon

Y'know, this is the stinking muck-heap into which unthinking business writers plunge with quite amazing regularity. NEVER use technical jargon unless you're absolutely certain that the recipient(s) of your work are privy to the beastly stuff.

Remember, also, that attempts to 'dress up' one's writing

with incestuous commercialese is a forlorn and hopeless endeavour; as witness:

the writer takes pleasure in reporting that

with reference to Part E of this report (*use* 'concerning', 'regarding', etc.)

assured the writer of their best attention at all times (*leave such cringing nonsense where it belongs, in Ye Olde Curiosity Shoppe*)

attached at Appendix 'A' please find (*use* 'see Appendix "A" '

owing to the fact that (*use* 'due to')

etc., etc.

Abbreviations

Similarly, NEVER use abbreviations unless you are certain that the recipient(s) will understand them. In cases of uncertainty, where a name is repeated several times within a text, spell it out in full at first and abbreviate thereafter, for example:

To set up the Personal Computer Word Processor (PCW), it is necessary to attach a plug to the end of the mains lead at the rear of the monitor unit. The PCW26 includes a keyboard, which is . . .

Punctuation

Adequate punctuation in written English serves two purposes, namely:

it ensures that the intended message is conveyed clearly and unambiguously;

it provides breathing spaces for the poor old reader.

So, it behoves us to pay more than a shred of attention to the individual use of some of the major punctuation marks.

• *The full stop* This signifies the end of a sentence, thereby allowing a full breathing space and, where relevant, a minor change of topic which doesn't warrant the start of a new paragraph or section, etc.

Incidentally, it's worth noting that the full stop was used widely (together with the comma) in the now old-hat system of writing known as '*closed punctuation*':

Flt. Lt. G. T. Pranger, A.F.C.,
12, The Maltings,
Puddlecombe Marsh,
Burble-on-Sea.

– as opposed to the cleaner, more modern '*open punctuation*' approach:

Flt Lt G T Pranger, AFC
12 The Maltings
Puddlecombe Marsh
Burble-on-Sea

, *The comma* The comma has a number of important uses:

(a)   to indicate a pause between sense groups of words, as in:

Picking up the paper he paused, thought for a moment, then scrawled his signature.

(b)   to separate words or phrases in a series, as in:

It will be necessary to include carbon paper, invoice pads, paper clips and six ring-binders in the order.

(c)   to insert a modifying or 'enlarging' phrase between a subject and its verb, as in:

The change, which had been quite unexpected, was welcomed by every member of staff.

(d)   to separate introductory words or phrases, as in:

Lastly, we have to decide who is responsible.

Having considered the evidence, I am satisfied that . . .

(e)   to separate short sentences joined by a conjunction where there is a change of subject, as in:

I have read your report, but you omitted to send me the full specification.

(f)   simply to provide a breathing space at a suitable point in longer sentences, as in:

I much enjoyed reading the final chapters of your

manuscript, and hope that it will not be too long before we see it in print.

Note that it's no longer a heinous crime to preface 'and' with a comma, as shown above. For all modern, practical purposes, it is those breathing spaces that count.

(g)   to punctuate large numbers, as in:

12,463   £28,000,000

; *The semi-colon* Although tending to fall out of fashion, the semi-colon is a useful device to indicate a pause which is longer than a comma, but shorter than a full stop; as in this sentence.

— *The dash* Some learned folk dictate that the dash should be avoided – but, as you can see from this book, I subscribe to the rebel school of thought. I offer that the dash is a most effective means of indicating a pause and/or an elucidation, as in:

He was an engaging character – pleasantly urbane and witty, to boot.

It can also be used as a handy substitute for brackets (sorry, parentheses), as in:

The dash – frowned on by many – is here to stay!

: *The colon* The colon is mainly used to introduce an explanation or a quotation, as in:

The reorganization has produced some distinct advantages: better working conditions, increased efficiency, more effective communications and, last but not least, a marked improvement in morale.

It was Jonathan Swift who wrote: Proper words in proper places, make the true definition of style.

,
The apostrophe This causes more than a few managers to run away with their punctuation. The apostrophe has a number of important uses:

(a)   to indicate possession, as in:

Singular   the manager's job
a year's salary

Plural   the managers' jobs
four years' salary

(b)   in contractions, as in:
      I have ››› I've
      it is ››› it's★

(c)   in *short* words ending in 's', as in:
          the boss's car
          Jones's appointment
      But watch out for those longer words ending in 's', as in:
          Mephistopheles' kingdom

Workbox 9

I think you deserve a bit of a break from the dull old textbook stuff, so here's a chance for you to jerk some life into those mental limbs with another workbox.

1   Many managers (and I'm one of 'em) suffer from that most dreaded of writers' afflictions, spelling heebie-jeebies. That being so and with due deference to you, reader, here is a selection of words which have caused headaches to umpteen writers over the years. *Some are spelled incorrectly* – pick them out and jot down the correct version in each case, will you?

accessible	accessory
accomodation	acquiesence
acquire	address
aggregate	aggressive
analysis	apalled
arguement	beneficial
benefited	chargable
committed	committee
contemptable	decieve
deferment	defered
definitive	develope
disappeare	diseminate
embarrasment	equipped
exagerated	fulfill

★ But never use an apostrophe when 'its' is used to mean 'of it'.

goverment	humorous
illegable	immoveable
inconsistent	insistant
intelligable	maintenance
manoeuvre	miscelaneous
neccesary	negligible
noticeable	occassional
occurr	ommitted
parallel	presede
proceedure	recieve
regrettable	resistent
seperate	sincerly
succeed	successfull
supercede	technical
temporary	unecessary

2   It's a dirty trick, but have a go at punctuating the following passage.

In Paris there is preserved a manuscript more than a thousand years old called Liber Ignium which may be freely translated as The Book of Fireworks the ancient writer goes to great lengths to describe various methods of using fire against ones enemies and among his collection of recommendations for the effective slaughter of fellow humans there appears one of the first recorded specifications for Man's original explosive brainchild gunpowder no one can say who first had the bright idea to mix saltpetre (75 parts) charcoal (15 parts) and sulphur (10 parts) together or for that matter what befell the unknown adventurer who first ignited the potent brew but it is known that the Chinese let off crackers on fete days many centuries before the birth of Christ Greek Fire an early derivative of gunpowder was a highly effective weapon of war and although the secret of how to make it has been lost it is supposed to have been composed of sulphur naphtha saltpetre and pounded resin it is said that not even water would put it out and that the Greeks used it in fighting the Saracens providing an early foretaste of the napalm bomb and lending weight to the old adage that there is nothing new under the sun it is described as capable of clinging to men and beasts eating its way through armour and setting fire to any ship on which it was thrown.

As usual, you'll find the tutorial at the end of this chapter.

Tutorial to Workboxes 8 and 9

Workbox 8

If you've done as teacher asked and made rough notes of where and how the respective writers went wrong, you are now in a position to correct their various transgressions. You'll recall that I asked you to look out for:

- expressions of personal views and/or prejudice;
- apparent irrelevancies;
- ill-organized presentation of component sections;
- lack of clarity/ambiguity;
- the use of needless jargon/commercialese.

All right, all you have to do now is pick the report body which contains the greatest number of revealed weaknesses – and *totally rewrite the thing*. If, perchance, it's very lengthy, I'll relent slightly – and ask that you persevere with several paragraphs. Remember, only you can decide whether or not you need to practise this aspect of report writing, so you're on your honour . . .

Workbox 9

1 Here is the list of words, with the misspelled versions highlighted and duly corrected.

accessible	accessory
accommodation	*acquiescence*
acquire	address
aggregate	aggressive
analysis	*appalled*
argument	beneficial
benefited	*chargeable*
committed	committee

contemptible	*deceive*
deferment	*deferred*
definitive	*develop*
disappear	*disseminate*
embarrassment	equipped
exaggerated	*fulfil*
government	humorous
illegible	*immovable*
inconsistent	*insistent*
intelligible	maintenance
manoeuvre	*miscellaneous*
necessary	negligible
noticeable	*occasional*
occur	omitted
parallel	*precede*
procedure	*receive*
regrettable	*resistant*
separate	*sincerely*
succeed	*successful*
supersede	technical
temporary	*unnecessary*

Okay, smartie-pants, so you got them all correct – or did you?

A word to the wise . . . If, like yours truly, you do happen to be pretty awful at spelling, you've probably got a dog-eared dictionary stowed near at hand. Why not reap a double benefit, spelling and word-wise, by supplementing it with a thesaurus – which, with its wonderful arsenal of synonyms, can be invaluable when one is searching frantically for an alternative expression or is simply at a loss for a word to fit a thought. Go on, splash out!

2   Your punctuation of this passage may not wholly coincide with mine – for, in this enlightened age, the rules governing punctuation are no longer well-nigh inviolable. However and hopefully, there should be a distinct similarity between our two versions, so get checking . . .

In Paris there is preserved a manuscript more than a thousand years old, called 'Liber Ignium', which may be freely translated as 'The Book of Fireworks'. The ancient writer goes to great lengths to describe various methods of using fire against one's enemies and, among his collection of recommendations for the effective slaughter of fellow-humans, there appears one of the first recorded specifications for Man's original explosive brainchild, gunpowder. No one can say who first had the bright idea to mix saltpetre (75 parts), charcoal (15 parts), and sulphur (10 parts) together – or, for that matter, what befell the unknown adventurer who first ignited the potent brew, but it is known that the Chinese let off crackers on fete days many centuries before the birth of Christ. Greek Fire, an early derivative of gunpowder, was a highly effective weapon of war, and although the secret of how to make it has been lost, it is supposed to have been composed of sulphur, naphtha, saltpetre and pounded resin. It is said that not even water would put it out, and that the Greeks used it in fighting the Saracens. Providing an early foretaste of the napalm bomb, and lending weight to the old adage that there is nothing new under the sun, it is described as capable of clinging to men and beasts, eating its way through armour and setting fire to any ship on which it was thrown.

6   Report conclusions, recommendations and appendices

O most lame and impotent conclusion!
William Shakespeare, *Othello* (II.i.161)

I don't know why, but many of us tend to get our proverbial knickers in a twist over report conclusions and recommendations. This can be a fatal chink in one's report writing armour –for, let's face it, these two components are the crunch sections of any report. Get 'em wrong and, in no time flat, the Ivory Tower carrion crows will be having you for breakfast . . .

So, reader, we'd better do something about it, eh?

Part A – Conclusions

For starters, take a mental pace backwards and ask yourself, what was Chapter 5 all about? And quick as a flash comes the reply – the body of the report, you idiot. OK, second question – can you think of another, probably more apt term for this most important section?

Well, how about the FINDINGS of the report? Think on't. By its very nature, a report presents a series of facts on a specified subject for a specified purpose, or, to put it another way, whatever the subject, it is wholly concerned with an *investigation* – and the body of the report presents a detailed account of the findings of that investigation.

All of which brings us face-to-face with the definition of the conclusions section: *it is a summing-up, or brief precis of the findings of the report.*

If, as I somewhat cheekily assume, you are not a skilled report writer, it's a fair bet that you'll have encountered some hiccups in the past when trying to formulate conclusions.

Your thought processes may well have travelled along the following, well-worn lines:

> *Right, that's the main bit done – now all I've got to do is dream up some conclusions . . .* [Chews the top of ball-pen to destruction while attempting to jerk the old grey matter into thinking mode.] *Hell, I've said all that has to be said – I can't just repeat myself . . . I s'pose what I really need is some super-impressive, 'different' kind of comments – something that'll cause 'em to rock back on their heels, kind of thing . . . But, WHAT, for goodness sake?*

But now you know, and it's worth repeating. If you wish your conclusions to impress, what you've got to do in each and every case *is produce a short, sharp resume or synopsis of your principal findings.* The whole purpose of the conclusions section is to provide the reader with a helpful gist of the various outcomes of the investigation under report – nothing more, nothing less.

And, yes, that can still be quite a task. D'you remember (of course you do) that checklist in Chapter 4 for compiling report summaries? Well, that series of tips can be of some assistance when weeding out and compiling conclusions – always provided that you bear your objective, that of seeking *findings* very much in mind. As we've noted earlier, the main body goes into pretty fine detail (the methods used to collect data or information, tests carried out, etc.), and none of this extensive, 'lead-up' material should appear in the conclusions.

Workbox 10

What follows is the body of a report. Read it carefully and have a go at compiling a suitable conclusions section – as usual, we'll compare results later on.

IV FINDINGS
A   The machine
   1 <u>Basic construction</u> Sir Hiram Maxim's flying machine comprises a central core and empennage, on which is mounted a biplane wing structure with an overall span of 104 ft, a dihedral angle to the upper planes and a total surface area of 4,000 sq ft. With the exception of

the mechanical components and certain other pieces of equipment, the flying machine comprises a skeletal structure, made almost entirely of wood (notably, spruce), with the planing and control surface frameworks enveloped in varnished fabric.

2 Motive power   The flying machine is powered by two steam-engines, each of 180 rated horse-power driving a propeller of approximately 8 ft in diameter. The engines, which are installed within the biplane wing structure, are gas-powered with a maximum recommended working pressure of 400 lbs per sq in.

3 Undercarriage   The flying machine is mounted on four flanged wheels which bear on a specially constructed length of railway track, gauge 7 ft 0¼ in. On outriggers it carries further flanged wheels which, once the main undercarriage has left the ground, are intended to engage with wooden guide rails raised approximately 2 ft above the ground on supporting stilts.

4 Control   Control of the flying machine is carried out by the driver from a position situated at a mid-way point on the central core structure. This driving position, which appears to be somewhat unprotected from the elements, is equipped with control levers which govern the movement of two elevators; one fore, one aft of the biplane wing. Further controls include the steam regulators and cut-offs, and the gas supply to the engines.

B   The test flight
1 Location   The single test flight was carried out at a meadow at Lowdean Farm, Bexley, Kent.
2 Date   The test took place at approximately 6.30 pm on 10th of July, 1894.
3 Object   The object of the test flight was to enable the machine to become airborne, but not take off altogether.
4 Description of the test flight
(a)   When steam had been raised and observers

stationed on each side of the track, Sir Hiram Maxim mounted the flying machine and, once he was satisfied that the propellers were turning at maximum revolutions, ordered those who were holding the wings to let go. The powerful screw thrust exerted by the propellers started the machine so quickly that some members of the handling crew, who had not let go as ordered, were nearly thrown off their feet. Watched closely by the writer, the machine appeared to bound over the track at an ever-accelerating rate.

(b) The first section of the track was laid up a slight incline, but, even so, the machine lifted clear of the lower, main rails and all of the top wheels were fully engaged on the upper track when about 600 ft had been covered. The speed rapidly increased, and when approximately 900 ft had been covered, one of the rear axle-trees, which were constructed of 2″ steel tubing, appeared to collapse. As a result of this failure, the rear end of the machine was set completely free and, rising to some ten feet above the track, swayed from side to side.

(c) At about 1,000 ft, the left forward outrigger wheel also got clear of the upper track and, shortly afterwards, the right forward outrigger wheel tore up approximately 100 ft of the upper track. It was at this point that Sir Hiram Maxim appeared to shut off steam to the engines, whereupon the machine sank to the ground and came rapidly to a standstill, with the main undercarriage wheels embedded in the turf. Sir Hiram Maxim was unhurt.

(d) The writer noted that, with the exception of the indentations made by the impact of the main wheels with the ground, the turf was unmarked. This evidence, coupled with his

> own observation of the test throughout its
> short duration, enables him to report with
> confidence that the machine was com-
> pletely suspended in the air prior to its
> return to earth.

Part B – Recommendations

The important thing to remember about recommendations is
that, contrary to an insidious belief, they're not always
required. In my time I've witnessed quite a few striving souls
who went bananas trying to cook up recommendations when,
quite plainly, such action was either totally irrelevant or
unnecessary. Needless to say, when a gaffer instructs a
subordinate to write a report, those instructions should
indicate whether or not recommendations are required. Sadly,
it doesn't always happen that way – so, if you're ever in any
doubt, ask.

The purpose of recommendations in a report *is to identify the
means by which a problem or situation may be resolved, so that
decisions may be made or appropriate action taken by those concerned.*
Therefore it follows as the night the day that they must be
sound in every respect – and here's a checklist to help you
achieve that state of grace.

Checklist for compiling recommendations
1   Examine the facts and the conclusions you have logically
    drawn from them. If all is well you should be in a position
    to know at the very least the gist of the recommendations
    you intend to make. The acid test is that the *reader* of your
    report should be able to anticipate the recommendations
    from your conclusions. It therefore follows that if *you*
    don't have a clue at this stage, something is drastically
    wrong with your presentation of the facts and/or your
    conclusions – in which case, whether you like it or not, it's
    back to the drawing board!
2   Ask yourself, are the recommendations you have in mind
    relevant to the instructions you have received? I'll say this,
    if they're at all wide of the mark, you had better have a

pretty sound justification for making them. Ensure that any such justification is included as a preamble to the recommendations themselves.

3   Having formulated them in your mind, ensure that each recommendation is recorded within the section as a separate item – we're back to that business of numbering/ referencing, again.

And that's it – so let's take a quick peep at some samples.

VI   RECOMMENDATIONS
    1   <u>Formula 35/C</u>
       The use of Formula 35/C should be discontinued.
    2   <u>Compensation</u>
       Adequate compensation should be paid to all person-
       nel who were involved in the laboratory development
       of Formula 35/C.

— — — — — — — —

F   RECOMMENDATIONS
In order to rectify the unsatisfactory situation summa-rized in Section E, above, the writer recommends that urgent consideration be given to implementing the fol-lowing measures:

(a)   all police officers should be permitted and en-couraged to use the rail system free of charge, subject to the production of warrant cards as and when required;

(b)   adequate publicity should be given to the action outlined in sub-para (a), above.

— — — — — — — —

5   RECOMMENDATIONS
    A   A training manager should be appointed and in-structed to implement a programme which will ensure that all personnel benefit from planned individual training and career development;
    B   The apprentice training scheme should be reintro-duced as soon as is practicable.

Workbox 11

Examine the following conclusions section from a typical report and, from the information available, use your imagination to formulate suitable recommendations.

D   CONCLUSIONS
The principal conclusions drawn by the Working Party were as follows:

(a)   the widespread criticisms by users of the existing transport were justified;

(b)   the current requirements placed impossible demands upon the transport staff concerned;

(c)   the vehicles in current use were in urgent need of replacement;

(d)   the transport section had expanded to the point where the existing supervisor could not be expected to maintain an efficient control over its operation.

As usual, we'll compare notes on this wee task at the end of the chapter.

Part C – Appendices

Is it really necessary, you may well ask, for me to deal with report appendices as a separate issue? Surely to goodness, there's nothing complicated about an appendix – it's merely something that, when the need arises, is tacked on at the end of the flippin' report, isn't it?

If that is your reaction, friend – well, fie on you. One of the biggest difficulties facing the average report writer (there I go again; who the hell is an 'average' report-writer?) is the burning question:

What should constitute an appendix – and what shouldn't?

CONFIDENTIAL

PERS/35/1/12/C

PROGRESS REPORT ON THE INTRODUCTION OF THE PRIVATE MEDICAL SCHEME

by

G B Simonds
Personnel Manager

For the attention of: 19 June 1989

Mr A R Wilberforce
Managing Director

CONFIDENTIAL

Figure 12(a) Part of a typical formal report – depicting, in conjunction with Figures 12(b), 12(c) and 12(d), the components covered thus far

---

CONTENTS

Figure 12(b)   Part of a typical formal report – depicting, in conjunction with Figures 12(a), 12(c) and 12(d), the components covered thus far

The basic rule is that data or information which is essential to the report should always be included within the body of the document, *provided it is not of a complexity or length which will sidetrack the reader's attention or hinder his understanding of the principal issues involved.* If the material cannot be said to satisfy this vital requirement, then the writer has no option but to include it as an appendix – remembering, of course, to tell the reader what has been done, for example:

> . . . As a result, the equipment was tested over a period of 120 hours' continuous operation, with pressure readings taken every hour (see Appendix A) . . .

It may be a very obvious point, but merely labelling one's appendices with indentifying letters or numbers is *not* sufficient – each such item should be headed with a clearly expressed, succinct title.

And now, for the last time, to the big yin

Figure 12 presents the final stage of our brick-by-brick, ongoing example of a typical report. Don't just let your glazed eyes slide over the thing – it's there for you to criticize *and* improve.

– 1 –

1   TERMS OF REFERENCE
The writer was instructed by the Managing Director to investigate the degree of overall success of the newly-implemented private medical scheme and to make recommendations, accordingly.

2   SUMMARY
(a)   Subject of the report   This report details the implementation and findings of a survey carried out by the writer to determine the extent to which voluntary membership of the private medical scheme had been taken up by employees and, *inter alia*, to assess the overall success or otherwise of the scheme.

(b)   Conclusions   It was concluded that since, as revealed by the survey, some 92% of those eligible had opted for membership and the Privamed Society had already actioned a significant number of claims, the scheme was operating successfully. As a result of widespread enquiries made during the survey, it was further concluded that the scheme was generally regarded as an important and much-appreciated employee benefit.

(c)   Recommendations   The writer recommends that the scheme be continued as presently constituted, and that eligible employees who have not already opted for membership should be individually counselled in relation to the many advantages offered by cost-free medical insurance.

Figure 12(c)   Part of a typical formal report – depicting, in conjunction with Figures 12(a), 12(b) and 12(d), the components covered thus far

– 2 –

3   INTRODUCTION
The private medical scheme, offering a wide range of free medical insurance benefits to all employees with over twelve months' continuous service, was introduced on 1 March 1989. Notwithstanding that the scheme enjoyed swift and general popularity, it was considered desirable that a survey be conducted in order to assess the degree of this success in more precise terms, and make recommendations accordingly. Tasked with this survey, the writer decided that it would be best achieved by a three-fold approach:

(a)   an examination of the available statistics on membership numbers and claims made during the first three months' operation of the scheme;

(b)   a series of interviews conducted with the aim of seeking the views of a representative sample of those employees who had enrolled for membership;

(c)   a series of interviews conducted with the aim of seeking the views of a representative sample of those employees who had declined membership of the scheme.

Figure 12(c)   *(continued)*

– 3 –

4 FINDINGS
  A Membership and Use of the Scheme
      (i) A survey of the personnel records revealed that, as at 14 July 1989, 564 employees had completed twelve months' continuous service with the company, and were therefore eligible to join the private medical scheme.
      (ii) Of this number, 518 employees (91.8%) had enrolled in the scheme.
      (iii) Figures produced by the Privamed Society (see Appendix 'A') show that during the period 1 March to 14 July 1989, inclusive, a total of 53 claims were received from members, of which 48 had been settled and the remainder were awaiting payment. When the rate of claims, some 10.2%, was queried, Mr H T Heslop, the Privamed representative, stated his opinion that, in view of the prevailing weather during the period, the figure could rightly be regarded as 'low-average'.
  B Members' Views of the Scheme
      (i) In order to gain a more accurate indication of the popularity of the scheme, a total of 52 members (representing a cross-section of the company, and comprising 4 managers, 10 supervisors and 38 clerical staff) were interviewed by the writer and the Welfare Officer. Of those interviewed, a total of 26 members had submitted claims, all of which had been settled by Privamed.

Figure 12(c) *(continued)*

– 4 –

(ii)   While due allowance must be made for the subjective nature of the exercise, certain specific questions produced responses as shown:

(a)   To what extent are you satisfied with the benefits offered by the private medical scheme?

Very satisfied	Satisfied
21	27

Minimally satisfied	Dissatisfied
4	Nil

(b)   Now that you know the annual cost to the company of the scheme, do you think this money should have been expended on some other employee benefit?

No	Yes
51	1

(iii)   (c)   (Addressed to the 26 members who had submitted claims.) To what extent are you satisfied with Privamed's handling of your claim(s)?

Very satisfied	Satisfied
24	2

Figure 12(c)   *(continued)*

– 5 –

C   Views of employees who had declined member-
    ship
    (i)   In order to gain a more accurate indica-
          tion why 46 employees had declined
          membership of the scheme, all concerned
          were briefly interviewed by the writer and
          the Welfare Officer. Of this total, 11
          employees stated that they had changed
          their minds and wished to join the
          scheme. The necessary applications have
          been completed in respect of this group,
          with membership to commence w.e.f. 1
          August 1989.
    (ii) Of the remaining 35 employees, 23 gave
          as their reason for refusing membership
          the fact that they were opposed to the
          principle of private medical treatment on
          political grounds. In the case of the
          remaining 12 employees, it was not pos-
          sible to establish conclusive reasons for
          their rejection of the scheme, but there
          were indications that some individuals
          thought that, as private patients, they
          would be 'singled out' from those under-
          going National Health Service treatment;
          and, as a consequence, would feel embar-
          rassment and/or social unease. However,
          7 of the 12 did state that they would give
          the matter further consideration.

Figure 12(c)   *(continued)*

– 6 –

5   CONCLUSIONS

    (a)   Since, as revealed by the survey, 91.8% of those eligible had opted for membership and the Privamed Society had already actioned a significant number of claims, it was concluded that the private medical scheme was operating successfully.

    (b)   Furthermore, as a result of the widespread enquiries made during the survey, it was concluded that the private medical scheme was generally regarded as an important and much-appreciated employee benefit.

6   RECOMMENDATIONS

    (a)   Subject to periodic monitoring of the service provided by Privamed, the private medical scheme should continue.

    (b)   Eligible employees who have not already opted for membership of the scheme should be individually counselled in relation to the many advantages offered by the Company's provision of cost-free medical insurance.

Figure 12(c)   *(continued)*

APPENDIX

PRIVATE MEDICAL SCHEME

**DETAILS OF CLAIMS
DURING THE PERIOD 1 MAR–14 JUL 89**

	Claims awaiting settlement	Claims settled
Consultations with GMP		
Visits to surgeries	5	34
Home visits	–	11
Consultation with Specialist		
Visit to Specialist	–	2
Hospital Admissions & Treatment		
Appendectomy	–	1
TOTALS	5	48

Figure 12(d)   Part of a typical formal report – depicting, in conjunction with Figures 12(a), 12(b) and 12(c), the complete example

And, yes, you now have to criticize and improve *your* completed report . . . .

Tutorial to Workboxes 10 and 11

Workbox 10

It'll not have escaped your eagle attention that this part-report has been compiled by someone who was an eye-witness to an event which took place a few years ago – on 10 July 1894, to be precise. However, the fact that, in drawing up your conclusions, you've been asked to take a trip back in time should not be a cause for complaint – for, after all, the principles of decent report writing are timeless, are they not?

Who knows, for the sheer fun of it, you may have been a complete sport and expressed your conclusions in the aspidistra-ridden style of that bygone era – but what we're concerned with is *what* conclusions you've drawn, not how they are written . . .

First and foremost, you suffered one disadvantage in that you were denied a sight of the *terms of reference* for this report. This means that you couldn't know exactly what the writer was required to report on – and thus you were inhibited in your task. However, on the evidence available, would you agree with me when I offer that the writer was almost certainly required to observe the test flight and report on its outcome? I hope so, because I believe one pretty solid conclusion is that Sir Hiram Maxim's flying machine actually flew – albeit for a very short time and in the style of a brick. We don't want to nit-pick over the point, but the findings do refer to the upper wheels getting clear of their track – *ergo*, for an unknown number of seconds, the infernal thing flew. And, as I've said, I believe that is the main conclusion to be drawn from the findings.

But did you come up with any others, perchance? How about the thrust of those socking great propellers and the lift then generated by the wings being sufficient to lift the main wheels off their tracks – because, according to our unknown reporter, that is what happened? And, just as a further instance, is there not sufficient evidence within the findings to enable one to conclude that the test was prematurely halted by the collapse of one of the rear-axle trees, whatever they were?

The whole point of this task was to prompt you into thinking about formulating conclusions – and if it succeeded in achieving just that, all well and good.

Workbox 11

I have no means of knowing what you've jotted down, but bearing in mind the general rule that one should be able to anticipate recommendations from the conclusions drawn in any report, my thoughts on this simple task are that:

1 the overall organization of the existing transport system should be improved;
2 the manning difficulties should be resolved;
3 the existing vehicles should be replaced.

It is, of course, likely that a 'real-life' report on such a topic would contain more detailed conclusions – with the consequence that the recommendations would also be more finely drawn.

A postscript on Bibliographies and Acknowledgements

Bibliographies

If it has been necessary within a report to refer to a number of other books and/or papers, it is helpful to the reader to include a short, sharp list of the items concerned. The standard procedure is to provide the following details:

Author's surname and initials – title of the work – name of publisher and year of publication.

The bibliography can be positioned in the report immediately before any appendices – remembering, of course, to note its presence and page number in the list of contents.

Acknowledgements

It is a matter of choice (unless, of course, the firm's policy dictates otherwise) whether or not to list those to whom gratitude is due for help in preparing the subject under report. There's one thing for sure, most people like to see their name in print, and an acknowledgement is certainly a good way of ensuring their help and assistance on future occasions. Again, position your acknowledgement(s) immediately before any appendices – and, once again, remember to amend that list of contents accordingly.

7   Something on multi-author reports

As writers become more numerous,
it is natural for readers
to become more indolent.
The Bee No 175, Upon Unfortunate Merit
Oliver Goldsmith, 1728–1774

While the hairy old adage that a camel is a horse designed by a committee may be open to some gentle ribaldry, there is very little doubt that many reports that have gone through the multi-author mill emerge as strange beasts, indeed. And, if you'll pardon the finger in your midriff, it's a point that I'm going to ram home.

By way of illustration, imagine for a moment that you've been able to farm out a reporting task to a bevy of the most proficient writers going. Having thus achieved the near-impossible, you proceed to give 'em a quick briefing – and then, because you value your skin, you head at a high rate of knots for the nearest cover. Why? Because, and you'd better believe it, you've brewed a recipe for potential emotional and literary disaster . . . Writing is not a science, it's an art – no less an art than painting or sculpture – and what you have done is require your acknowledged artists to unify their widely diverse styles and skills, eradicate individual and corporate writing warts – and, *olé*, come up report writing trumps. And that, measured by any standards, is a pretty tall order.

So, if that's often the situation when *gifted* writers are persuaded to take the plunge, what on earth are *our* chances of successfully negotiating the multi-author minefield? Well, take heart – for, provided one acknowledges that successful multi-authoring is a tortuous and risky undertaking, there is a way. Let's take a step or two along it.

First, though, here's a preliminary and very obvious idea for your consideration. If, as is usually the case, you are conscripted by the boss as the co-author of a report, it's more than likely that your fellow-writers will also be conscripts – and, uneasy partnership or not, you're stuck with it. On the other hand, if you happen to be wielding the big stick of authority and can afford some choice in the matter, then, for goodness sake, exercise your prerogative. Remember, it's possible to eradicate ALL the likely pitfalls of corporate authorship – by the simple expedient of recruiting someone to the group who, although ill-versed in the given subject, *is sufficiently good at writing to be able to produce a first-class report when fed the facts by t'others.* It's amazing how often this beautifully simple way out of the problem is completely overlooked – usually because very few people, and least of all the gaffers in our midst, give an ounce of thought to improving written business communication in any shape or form.

The make-or-break preparation bit

I think you'll agree that it's difficult enough for the members of any work group to maintain cohesion and work logically towards their goals – but, as I've already indicated, the imposition of a report writing commitment on such a bunch can really foul things up. Given all the inherent snags, the initial steps to lessen the odds against corporate success just have to be:

- ensure that the most all-round proficient member of the group is nominated or elected (and, breathing heresy, seniority may not be the best yardstick to go by where the former is concerned) as leader;
- then and only then, undertake ORGANIZED PREPARATION.

It was Rudyard Kipling who bequeathed the best possible advice to any report writer, but particularly those engaged in multi-authoring tasks, when he wrote these sterling words:

> I keep six honest serving-men
> (They taught me all I knew);
> Their names are What and Why and When
> And How and Where and Who.
> (*Just-So Stories*, following 'The Elephant's Child')

So, in the context of organized preparation for a multi-author report, let's spell out Kipling's Magic Six.

WHAT Are the group members entirely satisfied that:
(a) they know exactly what is required?
(b) if terms of reference have been allotted to them, that these parameters are sufficient in scope to permit successful completion of the task? If terms of reference have not been allotted, then these must be hammered out to the mutual acceptance of all concerned.

WHO *First*, who in the group is going to do what? It is not always the case that component aspects of the required report can be tossed happily into the laps of those who, by specialism or bent, are best qualified to take them on; for example:
(a) by so doing, will anyone incur an undue proportion of the work? If so, will the individual's day-to-day commitments inhibit successful completion, or should there be a rethink on the question of allocation of tasks?
(b) following on from (a), or for the reason that the group lacks certain required expertise, should someone else be brought in?
Second, who is required to read the report, and are they the right people? Are there any communication barriers which the group would be wise to take into account?

WHY The group should not allow the fact that they have been directed by someone on high to produce a report to blind them to the sixty-thousand dollar question: *why* is the thing necessary anyway? If you have ever worked in a bureaucratic organization, you will know that many hours of effort are completely wasted, merely because some damned idiot has uttered those deathly words:

'Ah, Carruthers – I, er, think we'd better have a report on this . . .'

HOW   In addition to establishing an overall *modus operandi*, it is at this stage that the group should determine all the aspects of report presentation which are pretty well bound to crop up; for example:

(a) what supporting material (i.e. appendices) should be included – and how will it be obtained/compiled?

(b) what diagrams and/or other illustrations are considered necessary – and how will they be produced?

WHEN   *First*, the group should consider any imposed deadline for completion of the report – is it realistic, or, more to the point, *achievable*? There are still those bosses around who regard the writing of a lengthy and complicated report as something that can be knocked off as a kind of executive afterbreath. Unless you are one hundred per cent certain that the priority for the beast is IMMEDIATE (and that is seldom the genuine case), insist that the group is given the time which it will undoubtedly require to produce a worth-while document. And, er, yes, I'd better go right out on a limb on this one. In the event that you're one of those unfortunate managers who strive to work as best you can amid conditions of frenetic, everything-wanted-yesterday disorganization, perhaps the advent of a scurrilously unrealistic report deadline should be the long overdue signal for revolt . . .

Second, there is the question of the group's self-imposed, achievable deadlines to be settled – who is going to complete what by when? It is in this area that the need for firm, fair and consultative leadership assumes paramount importance, for nothing can sabotage the team effort quite so effectively as the sluggard in its midst.

Third, when should the group meet to check on individual efforts, and progress in general? Failure to arrange interim get-togethers is an open invitation for the one and only, eve-of-deadline meeting to be scuppered by such plaintive cries as:

> *'But I didn't realize I had to do that . . .'*
> or
> *'You just don't appreciate the pressure I've been under – I haven't had a chance to complete it . . .'*
> etc.

WHERE   At first glance, this last of Kipling's Magic Six may seem totally irrelevant, but is it? Depending on the task, there may well be questions along the lines of:

> Where is this or that research or digging necessary to the successful completion of the report best carried out?
> Where is best for the group to meet?
> etc.

Having surmounted the initial, preparatory hurdle, it is be hoped that the individual members will retire to their respective, mutually agreed lairs and commence churning out well chosen and apposite words by the thousand. Oh, yeah? The group leader who takes refuge in that forlorn hope without routinely checking progress has got his or her executive head firmly in the *strato-cumulus*. So, leader, do your stuff – and that doesn't mean consistently hovering over their poor old shoulders like a bloody vulture . . .

And now we come to the hard bit.

Achieving a corporate writing style

I think I've already paved the way, as it were, for the central theme of this section – but, at the risk of upsetting your applecart, I'll lay it on the line. *It is tantamount to committing report suicide even to entertain the idea that Fred's, Mary's, John's and your own contributions merely require to be bundled together to form the final document.* Ah, was that a snorted I-know-that-already-you-idiot exasperation? Hum, well – why is it, then, that so many multi-authored reports reflect precisely such treatment? Hang the exasperation, let's grasp the nettle.

Someone in the group (very hopefully the person who, by virtue of sheer writing ability, is best suited to the task) has, by common assent, to assume the role of editor. A word, if I may, on the satisfaction of this apparently straightforward require-ment . . . I, for all my literary sins and shortcomings, am an author – and, as such, I'm totally convinced there's no way that my written outpourings should be let loose on the reading public without a modicum of sanitary treatment by my publishing editor – on whom, as I've often said in the best of Uriah Heep tradition, may the sun never set. Having stated thus, I must now make a frank admission. Nothing has made me madder than hell than when, as happened on two occasions several years ago, an editor slashed my so-called style of writing to pieces – and then proceeded to replace it with what, in my jaundiced view, was a mass of peurile, unreadable rubbish. On one of these occasions, my fury was amply justified; on the other, best-forgotten, occasion it wasn't – but that's irrelevant. What matters is that a number of us (or is it most of us?) tend to get very hot under the collar when someone else has the temerity to criticize a piece of writing with which we're very pleased, and over which we've sweated a fair amount of blood – especially when we've been praised for similar efforts in the past. So, the message is:

An editor must supplement skill with tact!

That said, we should now consider precisely what it is that the editor is required to do in dealing tactfully with the bevy of co-writers – for, believe me, it's tightrope stuff. In essence, the job consists of 'bringing up' and/or 'bringing down' the diverse modes, styles and qualities of the individual drafts to a common level; or, to put it another way, to produce a final document which, when read, will provide nary a clue that it has been produced by more than one author. This does NOT mean that the editor should seek to superimpose his or her personal style and what-not on the typescripts – we authors have a rightfully nasty word for such arrant malpractice.

What follows is a checklist of points that the editor of a multi-author report would do well to consider when checking individual contributions. By the way, I do not recommend that detailed editing requirements are aired at all during the group's preliminary get-together, since in my humble experience such an approach, however tactful, will often trigger dissension, doubts, or even downright fear where some of the members are concerned.

Please do not regard the checklist as exclusive – but, rather, as food for thought.

Checklist for the editing of multi-author contributions

Sequence	Are the facts presented in a logical order?
Omissions	Have any essential points been omitted? In this regard, a particular lookout should be maintained for neglected side issues and knock-on effects.
Clarity	Is the draft expressed in clear and simple terms? What about:

> ambiguity of style?
> undue use of jargon?
> pure verbiage and long-windedness?
> attempts at blinding with science?
> grammatical errors?
> spelling mistakes?
> the correct choice and use of words?
> have all abbreviations been explained by an initial application of each written in full?
> supporting detail in the context of appendices?

Diagrams, etc.   Are all the visual aids acceptable in their present form, for example:

> there is little doubt that, as with their writing, the quality and style of the individual contributors' diagrams, charts and so on will be at total variance – even if all concerned have been able to utilize a desktop publishing package. One of the editor's prime tasks should be to ensure that all such component parts of the report are standardized in terms of quality and style – ideally, by employing the talents of a single artist;

is each contribution relevant, or even necessary?

does each one convey the message it is intended to convey, and no more? The editor should seek maximum clarity by checking carefully for unduly complicated efforts – and, of course, discrepancies.

Finally, our hero's duty is to consider the crunch question: *does the edited report as a whole come up to scratch; in short, does it meet its objectives? There is bound to be the odd, unfortunate occasion when this will not be so* – usually when the deadline was yesterday and the editor is being harried for delivery. Whatever the pressures, the temptation to duck the decision to go back to the drawing board should be resisted – for there's no better way to ensure that the group will reap a whirlwind of displeasure than by submitting a bum report. Given such circumstances, one possible method of keeping the hounds at bay is to submit an interim document – which, let's face it, is a whole lot better than nothing.

8   Achieving the final professional touches

> Visually, this report has the semblance of
> an overworked midden – which, of course,
> could account for the stench.
>
> *Anon.*

Cast your mind back to Chapter 2 and, unless your memory is like mine, you may recall that I offered some tips on how best to set out and display your typewritten or word processed text. What we've got to do now is take this vital business of presentation several stages further – so, gird your mental loins for a fair old chunk of exactly that.

Part A – a brief introduction to report illustration

I can't guarantee that it was Confucius who said that a picture is worth a thousand words – but, whoever it was, he or she certainly said a mouthful. In fact, it's well worth labouring the point. Contrast, if you will, the bleary march of our eyes over great chunks of management reportage with the manner in which, often at a glance, those very same optics are able to take in a picture or diagram – and, with two all-important stipulations, we know the simple truth of the adage that *visual aids count*.

You'll hardly need reminding about the stipulations – but, hell, I'm going to spell them out anyway:

- whatever their form, illustrations must be *relevant*;
- and they must be *good*.

Having, I hope, gained your agreement that all but the shortest of reports should include at least one or two visual aids, we'd better examine the questions of relevance and quality in a bit more depth.

The relevance of illustrations

Do not succumb to the temptation of lightly dismissing as too obvious for words the relevance of illustrations – for, believe me, when it comes to deciding which bits in a report require illustration and which bits don't, it's often the case that the goose-writer's chosen sauce turns out to be anathema to the gander-reader.

For instance, if we're honest when we're compiling a report (and we've jolly well got to be), every once in a while it happens that our pen stops in mid-air – not because we're stuck for words, but because the sheer beauty-cum-quality of that last sentence or so, when compared with the rest of the beast, is quite outstanding . . . And because we regard this particular slice as the peak of our literary effort – bingo, it deserves, and gets, wholly unwarranted illustration.

But, for all that, our primary weakness is the failure to place ourselves in the reader's shoes:

(a)   consider, as objectively as possible, the reader's degree of familiarity with the area or topic concerned. Is this such that an illustration would facilitate his or her comprehension (for, after all, that is what you are seeking)?
or
(b)   is it the case that an illustration would need to be so complicated as to *detract* from the reader's understanding of what you have stated?*

The quality of illustrations

Quite probably, it's at this point that we come face-to-face with that nasty Catch-22 situation:

> Look, Goodworth, I accept what you say about the importance of illustrations in a report – but the truth is, I'm the world's worst artist . . . No diagram or drawing of mine, however simple, is going to do anything other than

---

* An affirmative response to this one can be a pretty good indication that the writer is up to the neck in the deep proverbial – in that the text itself has been poorly written. In this case, there's only one answer, it's back to the drawing board for a rewrite – utilizing simpler phraseology, more sectionalizing, etc.

DETRACT from my written work. I'd be asking for trouble . . .

If this particular cap fits, you have my sympathy – but that's all! The sad fact is that since your reporting life is bound to include many instances when illustrations are absolutely vital to this or that document, those illustrations just have to be of the highest possible standard – and if this means pulling in the help of someone else, this is what you're going to have to contemplate.

But let's not simply throw in the towel without a grain of thought, eh? The fact is that we're literally surrounded by a plethora of aids to effective, impactive illustration – and, if we're really keen to produce a better quality of work, it behoves us to climb off our butts and see what help is available. Stand by to do exactly that.

Part B – the quill pen approach to report illustration

Despite the burgeoning presence of electronic gizmos in our midst, there remains a legion of struggling report writers who cannot (or, in the case of the *laissez faire* merchants, will not) make use of modern technology. I therefore make no apology for kicking off with some pretty basic stuff.

When it comes to drawing pens, fings ain't wot they used ter be

Be honest, do – and acknowledge that your diagrams, or whatever, deserve more than a frenetic attempt to complete 'em with a chewed-up, splotchy ballpen, or equally disreputable stub of HB office pencil. Pop into any high street stationer and pick up one or two of the many liner pens that are now available, preferably of the 'hard plastic tip' variety. You'll never regret it.

Inability to draw a straight line?

. . . or, more precisely, lines at right angles to one another? If your artistic bent is similar to mine, all the rulers in the world will not prevent your umpteenth stab at drawing, say, a simple rectangle from looking more like a freehand sketch of a shipwreck. Obviously, where diagrams for a report are concerned, this very common hang-up spells potential disaster – but, y'know, there is an answer. Do as I did, and persuade the keeper of the petty cash that you need one of those small, desk-top drawing boards which, featured in all the office stationery catalogues, boast a built-in set-square (I think that's what it's called) and parallel rule. You can pay a fortune for such an item, but my latest catalogue advertises a very good one at under £35 – and I think you'll find it money well spent.

No good at lettering?

Well, fie on you. At worst, you can purchase a lettering stencil set – which, in my view and despite the advertising blurbs, requires some artistic skill and a hell of a lot of luck to produce good results. At absolute best, you can arm yourself with the odd sheet of rubdown transfer lettering – and, unless you really do possess ten thumbs, you'll find that your lettering is just what the doctor ordered. A few examples of the very many founts, or typestyles, which are available in rubdown transfer sheets are depicted in Figure 13. As you're probably well aware, they come in a wide variety of sizes (12 point, 15 point, etc.) and 'substyles' (solid colour, outline only, italicized and so on).

A good tip when selecting rubdown lettering is to avoid the sheets of very small characters, which can be absolute devils to space and line up. Simply go for a larger drawing with bigger letters and use the reduction facility on your office photo-copier to obtain the requisite size. An obvious bonus is that the reduction process will give your work that much-desired additional crispness of detail.

And lousy at sketching?

Admittedly, this can be a burden, but all is still not lost. There are a few publishers in the UK who offer books of

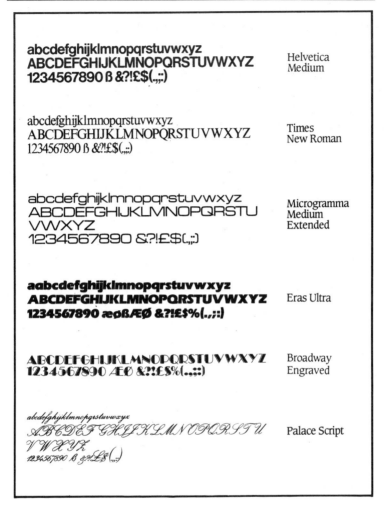

Figure 13 Some examples of the many fonts (typestyles) available in rubdown transfer lettering – and, for the benefit of the uninitiated, also in DTP software

copyright-free graphics – bags of drawings of everything under the sun, all of which have been produced with exactly this difficulty in mind. Figures, motifs, cartoons, borders, symbols, you name it – it's just a case of selecting the desired bits and pieces, photocopying them and including 'em within one's artwork.

Part C – Hey-ho for desktop publishing

Who the hell needs to be a skilled artist when, for moderate financial outlay and indulgence in a spot of practice, there are those millions of little pixels awaiting your every command? Thanks in the main to the protagonists of the home computer market, the days are now gone when desktop publishing (DTP) was the exclusive province of the well-heeled organization and even better-heeled individual – and this is splendid news for the ungifted amateur artist, like me and a zillion others.

If you have yet to plonk a toe in the paddlers' end of the computer pool, my advice is – don't be scared off. If yours truly can cope, so can you! For a minimum outlay of around £750 (it's up to you to decide whether the money should come from the family piggy-bank, or, albeit by dint of some persuasion, from the firm's coffers), you can acquire a computer and all the required software for word processing *and* DTP. Then, my friend, the report writing world is truly your oyster!

So far as reports are concerned, the massive advantage of DTP is that it enables one's work to acquire, after precious little practice, that invaluable stamp of professionalism. Aye, I know, one still has to face the oft-frightening nitty-gritty of stringing the right words together in the right order, dreaming up diagrams and what-not. But if one's finished reports are word processed (and, with the right software, electronically checked for spelling) and are supported by DTP-accurate, reader-friendly illustrations – boy, this helps.

However, if you or your boss either cannot or will not contemplate buying a word processing/DTP outfit, there remains one last resort – that of placing your work in the hands of one of the mushrooming high street businesses who, for a fairly moderate sum, will do all the magic dressing-up for you. And if that suggestion strikes you as wildly and expensively extravagant, consider this – if a particular report is important, if your *reputation* is important, then think again.

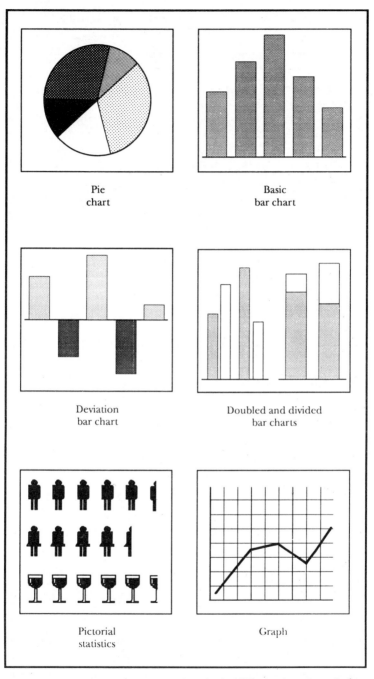

Pie
chart

Basic
bar chart

Deviation
bar chart

Doubled and divided
bar charts

Pictorial
statistics

Graph

Figure 14   Some basic examples of methods of illustrating numerical or
statistical information. YOUR job is to improve on these – in other
words, to INNOVATE

Part D – DTP or not, more on illustrations

First, reports are very often concerned with the presentation of figures – or, if you prefer the dreaded term, statistics. Figure 14 offers some very basic food for thought on the question of serving up such data in diagram form. Bearing in mind the inestimable truth of our core adage, 'a picture is worth a thousand words', don't be inclined to discard those words 'basic food for thought' unduly lightly. Figure 14 contains six examples – but, given a jot of brainstorming, it's possible to come up with a very great number of variations on a theme. Like everything else in business the name of the report writing game is innovation. Lest you doubt this or, perish the thought, you're disinclined thus to exercise your imagination, think on this – how many times have *you* seen a pie chart, a bar chart, or a graph of the type depicted in Figure 14 within the hallowed confines of a report, let alone anywhere else? The simple truth is, we've become so accustomed to seeing 'em that they've become hackneyed – and hackneyed stuff is boring stuff. So, get innovating, do!

Pressing on, Figure 15 depicts an algorithm, which is 24-carat jargonese for an idiot's guide to a given process. Contrary to many claims, algorithms were not invented by those who gave us programmed learning – they've been around since the year dot, and very useful they are, too. The one thing to remember is that an algorithm, like all other forms of illustration, should not supplant a chunk of text in a report, it should *supplement* it.

Continuing apace and descending for a jiffy to kiddies' primer stuff, I'm sure you know that any newspaper editor will give great attention to the headlines employed by his or her particular rag. And, yes, one of the reasons for this is all bound up with the business of catching the reader's eye; not, y'understand, merely to seek praise for artistic quality of work, but in order to get an essential message across, swiftly and bang-smack between both of those luminous orbs. Now take a look at Figure 16 which depicts a table with a nicely discreet but nevertheless effective 'headline' – a patch of shading which, in no time flat, will pass and impress upon the reader the message about warranty replacements for Model XB–20A components. In Chapter 2, I touched a bit more than

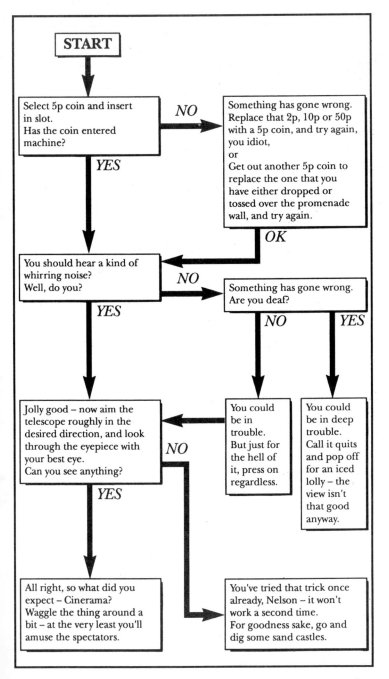

START

Select 5p coin and insert in slot.
Has the coin entered machine?

NO →

Something has gone wrong. Replace that 2p, 10p or 50p with a 5p coin, and try again, you idiot,
or
Get out another 5p coin to replace the one that you have either dropped or tossed over the promenade wall, and try again.

YES

OK

You should hear a kind of whirring noise?
Well, do you?

NO →

Something has gone wrong. Are you deaf?

YES

NO   *YES*

Jolly good – now aim the telescope roughly in the desired direction, and look through the eyepiece with your best eye.
Can you see anything?

NO

You could be in trouble. But just for the hell of it, press on regardless.

You could be in deep trouble. Call it quits and pop off for an iced lolly – the view isn't that good anyway.

YES

All right, so what did you expect – Cinerama?
Waggle the thing around a bit – at the very least you'll amuse the spectators.

You've tried that trick once already, Nelson – it won't work a second time.
For goodness sake, go and dig some sand castles.

Figure 15 A sample algorithm dealing with (just for a change) the operation of one of those seaside telescopes

MODEL	WARRANTY REPLACEMENTS JAN–JUL			
	MONITOR	PRINTER	KEYBOARD	CABLES
XB-20	3	–	1	–
XB-20A	8	11	5	–
XB-24B	2	–	4	1
XB-60	5	4	–	–
XB-60A	6	–	2	–
XB-60B	2	–	1	–
XB-80A	–	5	1	–

Figure 16 An example of the simple but valuable process of highlighting (e.g. headlining) an important message

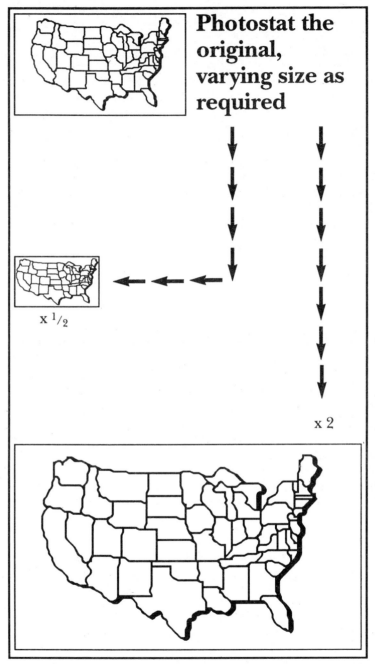

Photostat the original, varying size as required

x ½

x 2

Figure 17 One very obvious, but oft-overlooked, advantage offered by the photocopier

lightly (no pun intended) on ways and means of displaying, or *emphasizing* text – and, right now, the obvious message is that diagrams and charts *when required to depict something of importance* should also bear a crafty 'headline', as in Figure 16. Hey, I know I used the term 'obvious message' just then but, basic or not, it's a ploy that's often overlooked in the best of report writing circles.

I know I've already mentioned photocopiers in the context of reducing rubdown transfer lettering – however, in my experience, it's when one is striving to produce half-decent illustrations that these mysteriously-prone-to-breakdown machines really come into their own. You may think that I'm wallowing in the obvious, but the good old drill of cut, photostat and paste is often a splendid cure for the drafting doldrums – and, whether this is obvious or not, Figure 17 makes the point.

Part E – so much for the innards, what about the skin?

Thank goodness, my publisher (on whom may the sun never set) gives a great deal more than mere passing attention to the design of all his book covers – for, and here we go again with an obvious truth, it's the cover of a publication that prompts people like you and me to pick the thing up. Having stated this, I'd better add that I'm perfectly well aware that the workbound report writer isn't normally in the business of having to sell his or her work – which is probably one of the main reasons why reports, if they are graced with covers, are so often produced after the style of the one depicted in Figure 18. What's that I hear you murmur?

> Great balls of fire – give me patience . . . I know what you're getting at – and I don't like it . . . D'you really imagine that I've got the time, or the inclination, to spend hours designing a pretty-pretty report cover? And what d'you think the rest of the shower at work would say if I did? I'll tell you, 'Put his head on Goebbels' shoulders, and we'd have a right little creep.' That's what they'd say all right . . .

'Ave you done? While we're on the subject of time manage-ment, a good solid think on the way to work (assuming that

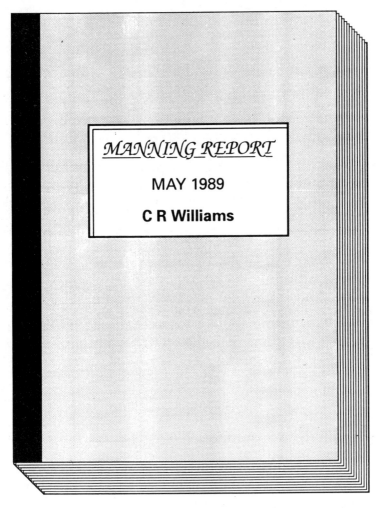

Figure 18 An example of the norm where report covers are concerned – neat, clinically economic and pretty uninspiring. Level of impact: say, 2 out of 10

you don't live there like I do, luckily) should do wonders on the subject of 'what' would make an *interesting, effective and impressive cover*. Given minimal skills and just a wee dollop of imagination, a 'hand produced' effort should take quite a bit less than, say, an hour-and-a-half's actual composing slog. Anyway, if you're one of the those worthies who are always talking about having to take work home, here's your chance to do exactly that. If, of course, you have access to DTP equipment – well, you probably wouldn't have got at me, in the first place. . . .

While it's undeniably true that your sudden emergence as a decker-up of report covers may cause widespread and even ribald comment among those honourable souls, your colleagues, you can take my word for it that much of this will stem from sheer, unadulterated envy – envy that they didn't think of improving their reports before you stole the march on them. I don't know about you, but I can stand that kind of envy – particularly when, in the jungle world of work, the rules of cricket seldom apply and any kind of 'score' is probably a lovesome thing, God wot.

But we're not interested in merely scoring, are we? The fact is that, given a modicum of effort, any moderately imaginative guy or gal can produce a more striking report cover than that shown in Figure 18, and here is a mini-indication of the truth of that sweeping generalization. Fairly recently, I persuaded three manager-students of my acquaintance to undertake a wee task, namely to design a cover for a mythical report. Having assured myself that these conscripted volunteers enjoyed little or nothing in the way of artistic abilities (the mere question was sufficient to prompt two of 'em to fall off their chairs laughing), I told them that this didn't really matter – because they were going to make use of DTP to produce their individual efforts. Initially, this caused a spot of anxiety, since none of them had previously dabbled in the process, but we got round this by means of short, sharp tutorials on which key to press in order to obtain this or that effect. Then, on three separate occasions, my helpful guinea-pigs were given two hours, maximum, to complete the task. I'd like you to see the results.

Alan's cover is reproduced at Figure 19. It's worthy of note that he copied the very small line drawing of the high-speed

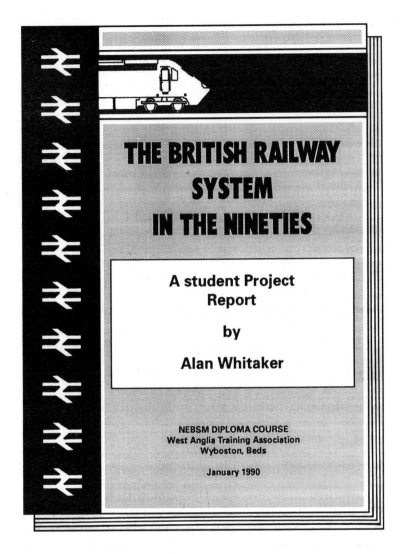

Figure 19 Alan's DTP-designed report cover

Figure 20   June's DTP-designed report cover

train's snout from a photograph, using the software's 'shape, rule and draw' facility – and he's justifiably proud of the result. I think you'll agree that he deserves credit for this very first stab at electronic design.

June wasn't completely pleased with her fictional cover, shown in Figure 20, but, once again, it clearly demonstrates what can be achieved with almost no experience of DTP. Her main self-criticisms were that the trick with the magnifying glass (also produced via the shape, rule and draw facility) 'lacked something', and that she should have moved the bottom block of print to a position where it centred directly beneath the 'Corporate Structure' block. For all that, it's a good *ab initio* effort, eh?

Bob chose to rely on the software's small library of ready-made pictures for his central theme, and the result is depicted at Figure 21. If that isn't a report cover with an impact, what is?

Part F – and this is the binding part

Let me start by making a plea; to wit, that you do not succumb to the old-hat and fearful habit of securing the pages of any decent-sized report by inflicting it with a staple stab-wound in the top left-hand corner. Anything just has to be better than that, so let's talk turkey about methods of binding and thus protecting your completed works.

Ready-made binders
Take a glance through any office stationer's catalogue and you'll find there's a massive array of ready-made folders, binders and fasteners from which you can select the type most suited to your particular requirements – ranging in price from the relatively cheap (and sometimes nasty) to the very expensive (and still sometimes nasty) so-called top-of-the-range stuff.

If I've managed to convert you to the tactical advantages of producing your own highly individual, impactive report covers, you'll maybe agree that it will not exactly help matters to shroud your work in the plastic anonymity of a ready-made

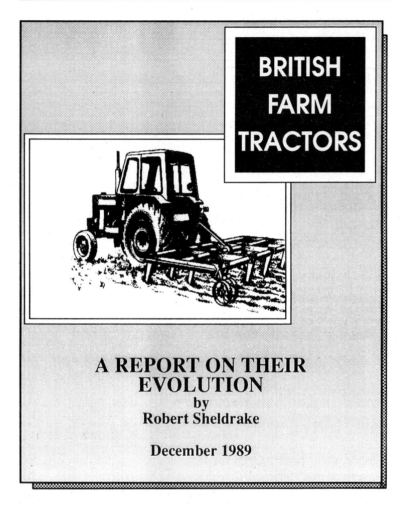

Figure 21   Bob's DTP-designed report cover

binder – unless, of course, it is one those transparent jobs, which are fine.

This whole question of binding and fastening is such a maze that I think the best thing I can do is to list some items by type – which, at the very least, will help you locate them in the index of that hefty stationery catalogue:

Slidebinders	Those plastic spines that, at the expense of one or two broken nails, one 'slides' on to the completed work.
Slidebind covers	Card or plastic sheets (they come in opaque and transparent form) to serve as covers.
Project covers	To name but one item – all with built-in fasteners. Remember to check the capacity of individual items – some accommodate up to 12 sheets of paper only. Other names for these are: display albums display binders boardroom files ring binders project files

Binding systems
These can be split into two categories: mechanical and thermal systems. The mechanical variety employs a hefty punch, which (given power to your elbow) perforates the work and then snaps a plastic gizmo through the holes, thus holding the thing together. The thermal binder takes the work in a vice-like grip, melts hot glue over the spine (and, if you're lucky, nowhere else), and then either mounts a protective cover over the glued area or leaves you to do this part of the chore. Yer pays yer money, yer takes yer choice!

All that now remains to be said is – happy and successful reporting!

Information bank – Part 1
The classification and analysis of data

The first step in classifying data is to organize it in groups according to a governing principle; for example:

information on aircraft may be classified by basic types:
Single-engined aircraft
Twin-engined aircraft
Four-engined aircraft
Gliders and sailplanes
(etc.)

while information on dogs may be classified according to their breeds:
Affenpinscher
Afghan Hound
Airedale Terrier
Akita
Alaskan Malamute
(etc.)

Thus, various governing principles, or criteria, could be applied when classifying employees within a particular organization, *but only one criterion can be applied at one time*; for example:
classification by department
classification by job title
classification by age
(etc.)

The important point to note is that classification into groups must cater for *all* the data or information – and thus it is that many classification lists include the item, 'Others'. Care should always be taken to ensure that the information entered under this heading is minimal in terms of its extent and/or importance, otherwise the value of the exercise could be severely eroded.

If and when it is found necessary to subdivide a group, it is equally important that the subdivisions cater for *all* the material within the group under further classification; for example:

Production department		120 employees
Managers	2	
Supervisors	5	
Section leaders	10	
Skilled operatives	43	
Semi-skilled operatives	57	
Cleaners	3	

In many instances it will not be possible or expedient to classify material because it is single by nature (a report on an employee's technical ability, a piece of equipment, etc.). Such material should be *analysed* – split up into selected parts which together comprise, as nearly as is possible, the whole.

Information bank – Part 2
Researching data at the library

The most common system used by libraries to classify non-fiction books (excluding biographies) is the Dewey Decimal System. In this system all such books are numerically classified in one of 10 main areas, each of which is then progressively subdivided in order to cater for an immense range of appropriate subsidiary subjects under each main heading. The table below shows the 10 main areas and their first subdivision.

000	*Generalities*
010	Bibliographies and catalogues
020	Library science
030	General encyclopaedic works
040	(Not yet assigned)
050	General periodicals
060	General organizations
070	Newspapers and journalism
080	General collections
090	Manuscripts and book rarities
100	*Philosophy and related subjects*
110	Ontology and methodology
120	Knowledge, cause, purpose, man
130	Pseudo and parapsychology
140	Specific philosophic viewpoints
150	Psychology
160	Logic
170	Ethics (moral philosophy)
180	Ancient, medieval, Oriental philosophies
190	Modern Western philosophy
200	*Religion*

210	Natural religion
220	Bible
230	Christian doctrinal theology
240	Christian moral and devotional theology
250	Christian pastoral, parochial, etc
260	Christian social and ecclesiastical theology
270	History and geography of Christian Church
280	Christian denominations and sects
290	Other religions and comparative religion
300	*The social sciences*
310	Statistical method and statistics
320	Political science
330	Economics
340	Law
350	Public administration
360	Welfare and association
370	Education
380	Commerce
390	Customs and folklore
400	*Language*
410	Linguistics and non-verbal language
420	English and Anglo-Saxon
430	Germanic languages
440	French, Provençal, Catalan
450	Italian, Romanian, etc.
460	Spanish and Portuguese
470	Italic languages
480	Classical and Greek
490	Other languages
500	*Pure sciences*
510	Mathematics
520	Astronomy and allied sciences
530	Physics
540	Chemistry and allied sciences
550	Earth sciences
560	Palaeontology
570	Anthropological and biological sciences
580	Botanical sciences

| 590 | Zoological sciences |

600	*Technology (applied sciences)*
610	Medical sciences
620	Engineering and allied operations
630	Agriculture and agricultural industries
640	Domestic arts and sciences
650	Business and related enterprises
660	Chemical technology, etc.
670	Manufactures
680	Assembled and final products
690	Buildings

700	*The arts*
710	Civic and landscape art
720	Architecture
730	Sculpture and the plastic arts
740	Drawing and decorative arts
750	Painting and paintings
760	Graphic arts
770	Photography and photographs
780	Music
790	Recreation (recreational arts)

800	*Literature and rhetoric*
810	American literature in English
820	English and Anglo-Saxon literature
830	Germanic languages literature
840	French, Provençal, Catalan literature
850	Italian and Romanian literature
860	Spanish and Portuguese literature
870	Italic languages literature
880	Classical and Greek literature
890	Literature of other languages

900	*General geography and history, etc.*
910	General geography
920	General biography and genealogy, etc.
930	General history of ancient world
940	General history of modern Europe
950	General history of modern Asia

960	General history of modern Africa
970	General history of North America
980	General history of South America
990	General history of rest of the world

Information bank – Part 3
Reported speech

If, when writing a report, it is necessary to record what someone has actually said, reported speech should be used.

The general rule for converting *direct speech* into *reported speech* is quite straightforward:

	Singular	*Plural*
DIRECT SPEECH		
First person	I	We
Second person	you	you
REPORTED SPEECH		
Third person	he, she	they

Here are some examples:

(a) I deny that I committed any offence.
    He [*or She, as appropriate*] denied that he [*or she*] had committed any offence.
(b) I think that this printer is just not up to the job.
    He [*or She*] said that, in his [*or her*] view, the printer was not suitable for the job.

In order to avoid ambiguity, it is often necessary to use names or identifying descriptions instead of, or as well as, pronouns; for example:

(a) He said that he was sure he had told Mr Carruthers about the accident.
(b) Mrs Hawkins stated that Mr Brownlow ought to apologize for his conduct.
(c) She thought that she, Miss Williams, was to blame for the error.

Tenses in reported speech

Note that in reported speech the tenses of verbs change; for example:

Direct speech	Reported speech
I try	He said he . . . tried
I am trying	he was trying
I tried	he had tried
I was going to try	he had been going to try
I have tried	he had tried
I have been trying	he had been trying
I had tried	he had tried
I shall try	he would try
I shall be trying	he would be trying
I shall have tried	he would have tried

The effect of time

Note also that because reported speech takes account of a lapse of time since the event(s) concerned took place, some words require to be changed; for example:

Direct speech
I think that everyone *here* this morning is in some measure responsible for *this* accident. I shall be speaking to all members of my staff *tomorrow* and shall tell them exactly how *these* new safeguards will affect their work.

Reported speech
She said she thought that everyone *there* that morning was in some measure responsible for *that* [*if not simply, 'the'*] accident. She would be speaking to all members of her staff *on the following day* and would tell them exactly how *those* [*again, if not simply, 'the'*] safeguards would affect their work.

Care with verbs in reported speech

Note, finally, that nothing makes a report more dull (and, in many cases, inaccurate) than the constant repetition of such expressions as, 'he/she said that . . .' The careful reporter will always strive to make use of alternative or more expressive (and accurate) verbs; for example:

> he stated that . . .
> she recommended that . . .
> he replied that . . .
> she urged that . . .
> she asked whether . . .
> he insisted that . . .
> he thought that . . .
> she confirmed that . . .
> she suggested that . . .
> he offered that . . .
> he remarked that . . .

Information bank – Part 4
Cliches and 'in-vogue' words

One definition of a cliche or 'in-vogue' word is that it is a hackneyed term or phrase. This usually means that it has long since lost the clear meaning which it once, if ever, had – and, albeit that this author is a constant offender, he must urge that the reader seeks to avoid their use. Here are some examples:

affluent society
at this point in time
breakthrough
comparatively (where there is no true comparison)
conspicuous by . . . absence
crucial decision
escalate
far be it from the writer to . . .
image (as in 'company image')
in real terms
in the foreseeable future
in the near future
in the very near future
in this day and age
it stands to reason
massive build-up
patently obvious
quite certain
reasonable
relatively (where, again, there is no true comparison)
the psychological moment
to a certain extent
to all intents and purposes
to be frank
unduly (where, yet again, there is no true comparison)

Information bank – Part 5
A glossary of key terms

Accountability   Responsibility for results or outcome.

Allocation   The quality or amount of a resource allocated for a particular use or purpose.

Amortization   Provision for the payment of debt by means of a sinking fund (i.e. money set aside for the purpose).

Appraisal   Assessment of a situation, performance, etc.

Arbitration   The referring of a dispute to an impartial body or person for settlement, with agreement by all the parties concerned to accept the decision made.

Assets   The items of financial value owned by an organization or person(s).

Asset stripping   The sale of the assets of a firm for a quick profit, instead of managing them to ensure growth and profitability. Asset stripping is often practised following a take-over.

Authority   Power – the right to utilize assigned resources within one's discretion in order to achieve given objectives.

Autonomy   The right and ability to operate on an independent basis.

Bio-engineering   The technique of designing artificial aids to life, e.g. life support systems.

Break-even point   The level of productivity or sales which is necessary to incur no financial loss or profit, i.e. to break even.

Budget   A financial statement specifying the maximum permissible amounts of categorized expenditure within a given period.

Capital expenditure   Expenditure on property, expensive machinery, etc., which, depending on its nature and market trends, will be recorded within an organization's accounts – and subjected to periodic financial appreciation or depreciation accordingly.

Capital-intensive   A capital-intensive activity is one in which capital accounts for a relatively large proportion of the activity concerned.

Cash flow   The flow of income and expenditure into and out of an organization. Net cash flow is the difference between expenditure and income.

Centralization   The concentration of an organization's decision-making processes within the upper echelons of the hierarchy, e.g. at group level rather than at subsidiary company level.

Conglomerate   An organization made up of a number of component organizations, all or most of which are engaged in different activities.

Containerization   A method of handling cargo in containers of standard size, each carrying up to 25 to 309 tonnes of items of different shapes and sizes.

Cost benefit analysis   A process of attributing money values to all the likely advantages and disadvantages of an investment project, so as to determine whether or not the project is worthwhile in a social and economic, as well as financial, sense.

Cost centre   Given component part of an organization which is responsible for certain stated costs and expenditures.

Critical path analysis   A technique widely used in planning major projects. The project is analysed into its essential activities, their interrelation is determined, and time is assigned to them. The resulting information is then displayed on a chart to highlight critical parts of the project which, if they were subjected to delay, could jeopardize the project as a whole.

Depreciation   An accounting process whereby the 'book value' of buildings, expensive machinery, etc. is depreciated on a periodic basis to allow for market trends, deterioration, obsolescence and so on.

Diversification   The production or sale of more than one commodity or service by one organization.

Division of labour   The specialization of workers in particular parts of a production or other work process.

Economies of scale   Savings that occur when output increases, so reducing the cost per unit of the goods produced.

Effective demand   The anticipated demand for a given product or service.

Ergonomics   The study of the relationship between workers and their working environment, also called human factor engineering.

Exchange rate   The price of one currency in terms of another.

Feedback   A principle used in self-regulating machines and biological systems whereby information about what is happening is fed back to a central point.

First-line or front-line management   Those who are directly responsible for the control and supervision of, say, shopfloor workers. This means that, despite widespread old-hat views to the contrary, supervisors and foremen, forewomen, etc. are managers – and should be included within the so-called management team.

Fiscal policy   The control of the growth or contraction of a nation's economy by the management of taxation and government expenditure.

Floating currency   The exchange rate of one currency in terms of another is subject to the forces of supply and demand, unless monetary authorities intervene to influence those forces. If there is no such intervention, the exchange rate of a currency is said to float, or find its own level. If there is then an increase in demand for the currency, the rate rises, and if there is a decrease in demand, it falls.

Fringe benefits   Any *non*-financial benefits received from an employer, in addition to pay.

Funding   The practice of converting short-term debt into long-term debt by the issue of long-term securities.

Goodwill   The difference between the sum of the value of the individual assets of a business and the value of those assets as part of a going concern (when the benefits of established customers and links with suppliers are quantified).

Human factor engineering   See *Ergonomics*.

Innovation   The introduction of new processes, procedures, concepts, etc.

Interest group   A group of people who have banded together in order to pursue a given objective.

Inventory   The supply or stock of resources on hand at any one time.

Job description   A statement of the main duties and responsibilities that are inherent in a given job.

Lateral mobility   The ability to move from one area of a

business to another, e.g. from production to sales.

Lead time The period of time that must pass between a decision being made and its coming to fruition.

Linear programming An operations research technique that can be used to determine the proper mix of products, etc. to maximize profits or some other given dimension.

Line management Members of management who are directly concerned with the primary function(s) of a business, e.g. production.

Liquid assets Those assets which can be turned readily into cash.

Macro-economics Study of the broad themes of economics that affect an economy as a whole.

Mass production The manufacture of a given product in large quantities at a rapid rate, and hence at a low cost per unit.

Matrix organization An organization mode wherein some employees are responsible for task and/or function assignments in more than one part of the organization at one time.

Micro-economics Study of the smaller, individual elements that comprise an economy.

Minimum lending rate The rate of interest at which the Bank of England lends money to discount houses and to the rest of the banking system. Commercial lenders gear their interest rates to the minimum lending rate.

Network analysis A method of analysis used in planning and scheduling, such as critical path analysis.

Operations research The study of the application of mathematical tools and logic to the solution of industrial problems.

Programme Evaluation Review Technique (PERT) A planning process that uses charts to aid in planning a project and evaluating progress when the project is under way.

Planned obsolescence An approach to design which is based on the expectation that the eventual product will become obsolescent or incapable of performing its function earlier than necessary, thereby facilitating the introduction of new products. Alternatively, the approach can be based on the expectation that the eventual product will become out of vogue before it is actually unusable.

Primary sector The agricultural, fishing, mining, quarrying, oil and gas industries, which provide food, fuel and raw materials.

Prime costs   Expenses which can be attributed to any single unit of a particular product.

Productivity bargaining   The process of negotiation between management and labour whereby increases in pay are granted in return for increased productivity.

Profit centre   Given component part of an organization which is responsible for its operations in terms of profit and loss.

Prototype   A pre-production model of a potential new product, used for evaluation purposes.

Qualitative factors   The factors to be incorporated in the decision-making process that cannot be quantified, such as subjective values and beliefs.

Rationalization   A process of concentrating a work activity into fewer units in order to secure more efficient use of resources. Sadly, as many employees know to their cost, rationalization is a term subject to much misuse.

Restrictive practice   An industrial practice restraining the free play of supply and demand forces, designed to obtain higher incomes or profits for those using it.

Secondary sector   The manufacturing and production industries.

Span of control   The number of persons who report directly to a given manager.

Strategic planning   The planning for an organization's long-term future in terms of identifying/setting major objectives, the basic methods by which the objectives will be pursued, and the means of obtaining the resources required.

Tertiary sector   The service industries, including those engaged in distribution.

Time and motion studies   The process of observing and timing work operations in order to break tasks into segments – which are then redesigned in order that they may be performed more effectively (ideally, in less time), thereby improving production.

Wage differentials   Differences in pay between different groups of employees which those in the higher-paid groups try to maintain whenever pay negotiations are in force.

Information bank – Part 6
Abbreviations – management/business (etc.) terms

When considering the use of abbreviations within a report, always remember the 'play safe' rule – at first, spell the thing out in full (capping the words with the abbreviation in brackets), and then resort to abbreviated references thereafter.

ab init	(*ab initio*) from the beginning
A/C, a/c	account
ACA	Associate of Institute of Chartered Accountants
ACAS	Advisory, Conciliation and Arbitration Service
ADC	*aide-de-camp*
ad fin	(*ad finem*) towards the end
ad init	(*ad initium*) at the beginning
ad lib	(*ad libitum*) to the extent desired
advt	advertisement
APP/App	appendix
ARIBA	Associate of the Royal Institute of British Architects
assoc	association
asst	assistant
BA	Bachelor of Arts
BCL	Bachelor of Civil Law
b/d	brought down
b/f	brought forward
BL	Bachelor of Law
B/L	bill of lading
BMA	British Medical Association
bros	brothers
BSc	Bachelor of Science
BSI	British Standards Institution
BST	British summer time
CA	Chartered Accountant

CBI	Confederation of British Industry
CBT	Computer based training
c/d	carried down
c & f	cost and freight
c/f	carried forward
ChB	Bachelor of Surgery
cif	cost, insurance and freight
CNAA	Council for National Academic Awards
c/o	care of
COD/cod	cash on delivery
CPA	critical path analysis
Cr/cr	credit or creditor
CRE	Commission for Racial Equality
CV/cv	curriculum vitae
DCF	discounted cash flow
DCL	Doctor of Civil Law
DD	Doctor of Divinity
dept	department
DHSS	Department of Health and Social Security
Dip	Diploma
DLit	Doctor of Literature
DM	Doctor of Medicine
DMus	Doctor of Music
DoE	Department of Employment
DP	data processing
DPhil	Doctor of Philosophy
DR/dr	debit or debtor
DSc	Doctor of Science
EAT	Employment Appeals Tribunal
E&OE	errors and omissions excepted
EDP	electronic data processing
EEC	European Economic Community
EFTA	European Free Trade Association
eg	(*exempli gratia*) for instance
EMAS	Employment Medical Advisory Service
EMIP	equivalent mean investment period
EOC	Equal Opportunities Commission
et seq	(*et sequentia*) and what follows
EWS	Experienced Worker Standard
faa	free of all average
fas	free alongside ship

FCA	Fellow of the Institute of Chartered Accountants
FIA	Fellow of the Institute of Actuaries
fob	free on board
for	free on rail
fpa	free of particular average
FRCP	Fellow of the Royal College of Physicians
FRCS	Fellow of the Royal College of Surgeons
FRIBA	Fellow of the Royal College of British Architects
FRS	Fellow of the Royal Society
GATT	General Agreement on Tariffs and Trade
GP	General Practitioner
HCF	highest common factor
HMSO	Her Majesty's Stationery Office
Hon Sec	Honorary Secretary
HP	hire purchase
HSE	Health and Safety Executive
HT	high tension
ibid	(*ibidem*) in the same place
ie	(*id est*) the same
ILO	International Labour Organization
IMF	International Monetary Fund
Inc	Incorporated
inst	(instant) in the present month
IPM	Institute of Personnel Management
iq	(*idem quod*) the same as
IQ	intelligence quotient
IS	Industrial Society
IT	Industrial Tribunal
ITA	Independent Television Authority
ITB	Industrial Training Board
ITV	Independent Television
JD	job description
JIC	Joint Industrial Council
lc	lower case
LCM	lowest common multiple
LDS	Licentiate in Dental Surgery
LEA	Local Education Authority
LittD	Doctor of Letters
LLB	Bachelor of Laws
LLD	Doctor of Laws
loc cit	(*loco citato*) in the place quoted

log	logarithm
LRCP	Licentiate of the Royal College of Physicians
LRCS	Licentiate of the Royal College of Surgeons
ls	(*locus sigilli*) the place of the seal
Ltd	limited liability company
MA	Master of Arts
MB	Bachelor of Medicine
MBA	Master of Business Administration
MBO	management by objectives
MCA	Management Consultants' Association
MD	Doctor of Medicine
MO	mass observation
MPS	Member of the Pharmaceutical Society
MR	Master of the Rolls
MRCP	Member of the Royal College of Physicians
MRCS	Member of the Royal College of Surgeons
MS	manuscript
MSc	Master of Science
MSL	mean sea level
MSS	manuscripts
MT	motor transport
MV	motor vessel
NATO	North Atlantic Treaty Organisation
NB	(*nota bene*) note well
NCB	National Coal Board
nd	no date
NEDC	National Economic Development Council
NHS	National Health Service
NI	National Insurance
No/no	number
Nos/nos	numbers
NPV	no par value
ob	(*obiit*) died
op	out of print, over proof
OPB	Occupational Pensions Board
op cit	(*opere citato*) in the work stated
pa	per annum
PAYE	pay as you earn
PBR	payment by results
pc	per cent
pd	paid

PE	physical education
P/E	price/earnings ratio
PER	Professional & Executive Recruitment
PERT	project evaluation review techniques
PhD	Doctor of Philosophy
pp	per pro
PPC	(*pour prendre congé*) to take leave
PPI	policy proof of interest
PPS	Parliamentary Private Secretary
PRO	Public Records Office, Public Relations Officer
pro tem	(*pro tempore*) for the time
prox	(*proximo*) in the next month
pto	please turn over
QA	quality assurance
QB	Queen's Bench
QBD	Queen's Bench Division
QC	Queen's Counsel
QWL	quality of working life
RD	refer to drawer
recd	received
rpm	revolutions per minute
RPM	retail price maintenance
RRP	recommended retail price
RSVP	(*répondez s'il vous plaît*) please answer
Ry	railway
ScD	Doctor of Science
SERPS	State Earnings Related Pension Scheme
sf	(*sub finem*) towards the end
SO	Stationery Office
Soc	Society
sp gr	specific gravity
SS	screw steamer, steamship
SSP	Statutory Sick Pay
STD	subscriber trunk dialling
St Ex	Stock Exchange
stg	sterling
subst	substitute
sup	(*supra*) above
suppl	supplement
temp	(*tempore*) in the period of
TO	turn over

Treas	Treasurer
trng	training
trs	transpose
TUC	Trades Union Congress
uc	upper case
ult	(*ultimo*) in the last month
UN(O)	United Nations (Organisation)
up	under proof
v	(*vide*) see, (*versus*) against
VDU	visual display unit
viz	(*videlicet*) namely
WEA	Workers' Education Association
wf	wrong font
WHO	World Health Organisation
WIP	work in progress
x-cp	ex-coupon
xd/x-div	ex-dividend
x-i	ex-interest

Information bank – Part 7
Abbreviations – weights and measures, etc.

Length

inch(es)	in
foot/feet	ft
yard(s)	yd(s)
mile(s)	mile(s)
millimetre(s)	mm
centimetres	cm
metre(s)	m
kilometre(s)	km

Weight

ounce(s)	oz
pound(s)	lb(s)
stone	stone
hundredweight(s)	cwt
ton(s)	ton(s)
gram(s)	g
kilogram(s)	kg
tonne(s)	tonne(s)

Area

square inch(es)	sq in
square foot/feet	sq ft
square yard(s)	sq yd(s)
acre(s)	acre(s)
square centimetre(s)	cm^2
square metre(s)	m^2

hectare(s)   hectare(s)
square kilometre(s)   km^2

Volume and Capacity

cubic inch(es)   cu in
cubic foot/feet   cu ft
cubic yard(s)   cu yd(s)
fluid ounce(s)   fl oz
pint(s)   pint(s)
gallon(s)   gall(s)
cubic centimetre(s)   cm^3
cubic metre(s)   m^3
litre(s)   litre(s)

Time

second(s)   s
minute(s)   m
hour(s)   hr(s)

Velocity

kilometres per hour   kph
metre per second   m/s
miles per hour   mph

Temperature

degree Celsius   °C
degree Fahrenheit   °F

Electricity

ampere(s)   A
volt(s)   V
watt(s)   W

kilowatt(s)   kW

Prefixes, etc.

mega	M
kilo	k
hecto	h
deca	da
deci	d
centi	c
milli	m
micro	μ
greater than	›
less than	‹

Information bank – Part 8
Recommended reading

Banks, J. G. (1966). *Persuasive Technical Writing*. Oxford: Pergamon Press.

Flesch, R. (1962). *The Art of Readable Writing*. Canada: Collier-Macmillan.

Gowers, Sir Ernest. (1948). *The Complete Plain Words*. London: HMSO.

Gowers, Sir Ernest. (1951). *ABC of Plain Words*, London: HMSO.

Grieves, R. and Hodge, A. (1967). *The Reader Over Your Shoulder*. London: Cape.

Jordan, S. (1971). *Handbook of Technical Writing Practices,* vols. 1 & 2. London: John Wiley/Interscience.

Vallins, G. H. (1951). *Good English – How to write it*. London: Pan.

Index